MAD, BAD
AND DANGEROUS

MAD, BAD AND DANGEROUS

THE ECCENTRICITY OF TYRANTS

Tom Ambrose

PETER OWEN
LONDON AND CHICAGO

PETER OWEN PUBLISHERS
81 Ridge Road, London N8 9NP

Peter Owen books are distributed in the USA and Canada by
Independent Publishers Group/Trafalgar Square
814 North Franklin Street, Chicago, IL 60610, USA

First published in Great Britain 2015 by
Peter Owen Publishers

PAPERBACK ISBN 978-0-7206-1447-3
EPUB ISBN 978-0-7206-1871-6
MOBIPOCKET ISBN 978-0-7206-1872-3
PDF ISBN 978-0-7206-1873-0

Typeset by Octavo Smith Publishing Services

Printed and bound in Great Britain by
CPI Group (UK) Ltd, Croydon, CR0 4YY

CONTENTS

INTRODUCTION

This book is an attempt to define the character of tyrants, a subject that has been of pressing interest in societies since the time of the Ancient Greeks. Over centuries methods of tyranny have evolved but the motive of the tyrant himself has remained constant. This motive is to achieve a position of pre-eminence in which he can assert his own will and self-perception over the rights and interests of the people. The popular image of the tyrant as a monstrous fiend has been encouraged by story and film – for example, the depiction of Ivan the Terrible in Eisenstein's great film. Yet the modern tyrant has evolved from Gothic monster to soberly dressed bureaucrat. This made the bizarre appearance and dress sense of the late Muammar Gaddafi all the more startling.

As paranoid and sadistic as the tyrant may have been, he still depended on popular support, even if it was manufactured by bribery and intimidation. Always at centre stage, the tyrant encouraged myths and created a false 'reality' around himself. The desired image was that of a good and supremely powerful leader who acted in the best interests of his people. They, in turn, were expected to love him without question. There is an almost childlike quality to this scenario, perhaps explained by the fact that many tyrants suffered a bullied and unhappy childhood themselves. The deprived infant became the adult bully, while denying that he had done anything wrong. The tyrant oppresses the people and then pleads innocence.

There is a theory that tyrants are just ordinary psychopaths, repeatedly performing immoral acts and exhibiting deceitfulness, impulsivity and lack of remorse. Certainly tyrannical rulers throughout history have all exhibited these traits, not only lying to others but deceiving themselves. As the historian Robert Service has written, 'If ever Stalin called somebody a traitor, it was not only the minds of others he was manipulating.' Similarly Muammar Gaddafi truly believed that opposition to his regime equated with hostility to the very existence of Libya. He consoled himself with the thought that, fortunately, the people were with him and that they were even prepared to die for him. This certainty that one's self-belief was justified led Adolf Hitler to refuse the contemporary equivalent of hundreds of millions of dollars to reclassify a small group of Jewish Austrians as non-Jews. Similarly the current Iranian regime's rejection of substantial offers of aid to end its nuclear programme was made because of a belief in the 'sacred value' of independence – which was considered more important than any practical gain.

While most democratic leaders employ subordinates who are empowered to question their actions, the tyrant rejects any such interference. As time passes, absolute power increases the isolation and eccentricity. A typical example was Mao Tse-tung, who remained in power for decades and whose abuses increased as he became ever more isolated from the people. Such men also lose their ability to see themselves and their relationships to others realistically. Supreme power alters the psychological make-up of those who possess it. Tyrants have always been happy to take credit for the accomplishments of others and begin seeing the world around them in a more simplistic way. This effect, according to some neurologists, is due to a serious malfunction of the paralimbic cortex – where our emotions are processed and where our sense of self-control lies.

Another theory to explain the eccentricities of tyrants is that they are more or less normal people who develop mental disorders in the extraordinary circumstance of holding absolute power. Tyranny is usually thought of as being the cruel and oppressive exercise of power, but the original definition of the term was rule by persons who lack legitimacy – whether they be malign or benevolent. Historically tyrants have tended to be insecure people who attempt to maintain power by becoming increasingly oppressive. Initially benign, they are still inherently dangerous. The best defence against them is to demand accountability to the people through the use of a written constitution.

A confluence of genes creates personality disorders such as narcissism, paranoia and anti-socialism, insists Professor Coolidge of the University of Colorado, who has profiled Kim Jong-il, Saddam Hussein and Adolf Hitler. Sons of dictators such as Kim Jong-un (son of Kim Jong-il) or Bashar al-Assad (son of Hafez al-Assad) are encouraged by their environment to maintain or extend their power. There are no reluctant tyrants, and once in power they are hard to dislodge because of their ruthless attitude to opposition. Power corrupts, as Lord Acton famously pointed out, and absolute power corrupts absolutely. Power also eases the stresses of daily life; powerful people – including tyrants – have lower levels of cortisol, a hormone closely associated with stress, than ordinary people. Lower cortisol also provides the tyrant or dictator with an abundance of emotional and cognitive resources to use when navigating stresses as they arise. In this way tyrants may become immune to regret.

Research at Columbia University also found that study participants who were placed in large offices and informed that they were managers made difficult decisions much more easily than those given the role of subordinates. Not only did the high-power group score lower on psychological measures of stress; they also had lower levels of cortisol in saliva samples. It seems the normal brain is not designed to wield absolute power. The reason why dictators fight to the end is because they do not understand the concept of 'end'. Gaddafi should have stood down before he lost everything; Mubarak should have left Egypt weeks before he resigned; Hitler could have brokered for peace and Saddam Hussein bargained for his life. But dictators are too strong militarily and too weak psychologically to bargain.

1

IDENTIFYING THE TYRANT

T yrants are born, not made. From the beginning they are driven by a disordered personality that does not relate to others, profit from experience, understand justice or maintain meaningful personal relationships. A recent example of such a personality was the late Colonel Muammar Gaddafi of Libya. The problem with Gaddafi was the difficulty of deciding whether he was a brutal dictator or just a lovable rogue misunderstood by international opinion. The strange costumes he chose to wear made the decision even more difficult. Gaddafi often appeared dressed like an illustration in a cartoon book of an outrageous comic tyrant. Many thought his chosen appearance was his way of mocking the West, arguing that no one would seriously make themselves look like a pantomime villain. His behaviour often complemented his appearance, whether he was haranguing a local audience or appearing at international conferences. The world observed such performances with amusement, and even when he was shown to be supporting global acts of terrorism Westerners still maintained a soft spot for the old rogue.

The true nature of Muammar Gaddafi was revealed soon after he came to power in 1969. It was the start of what would be a lengthy and efficient tyranny, administered through a series of revolutionary committees. Their task was to eliminate all internal opposition to Gaddafi. They were aided by a comprehensive spy network as efficient as any in modern history. The result was that 20 per cent of Libyans spied on the other 80 per cent. Neighbours betrayed neighbours, schoolchildren informed on their teachers. Anyone attempting opposition to Gaddafi's rule was arrested, and executions and mutilations were conducted in public and shown live on state television. This received little attention from the rest of the world, which considered the Colonel more of a curiosity than a threat to peace. But anyone bothering to follow his rambling speeches would have spotted one of the characteristics of the megalomaniac tyrant. During one of his early diatribes, which ran on for several hours, he stated unambiguously, 'I am an international leader, the dean of the Arab rulers, the king of kings of Africa and the imam of Muslims, and my international status does not allow me to descend to a lower level.' Eventually the US media reported his words, leading to President Ronald Reagan describing him as the 'mad dog of the Middle East'.

Over the next four decades Gaddafi did little to dispel the nickname, as his wild orations and writings interspersed his involvement in acts of world terrorism. By 1975 he was ready to summarize his political philosophy in a single book. This was his version of Hitler's *Mein Kampf* or Mao's 'Little Red Book', but in Gaddafi's case it was green rather than red and modestly subtitled *The Solution to the Problems of Democracy: The Social Basis to the Third Universal Theory*. The need to produce a 'bible' containing one's political philosophy and agenda for the world is another of the characteristics of tyrants throughout the ages. This was a fact recognized by the Ancient Greeks who took great pains to try to identify potential tyrants in their midst before they could seize power.

The problem was that the public often admired and supported tyrants because at least they got things done for the benefit of the people and against the wishes of the powerful elite of society. Among the first such tyrants was Peisistratos of Athens, who ignored both the laws and the constitution. His reign, like that of so many later tyrants, was characterized by substantial public works – the first to have been carried out in Athens for hundreds of years. Large temples and altars were constructed for Zeus Olympios, Apollo Pythios and the Twelve Gods. In addition, an extensive system of aqueducts and fountains were built, bringing a much-needed and reliable supply of clean water into the city. In spite of the good works the accompanying repression was too much for the Athenians, and Peisistratos' successor – his son Hippias – was driven from power around 510 BC. Hippias' successor was Cleisthenes, who reintroduced a form of democracy that reached its apotheosis fifty years later under Pericles. From now on all political decisions were taken by the 'Council of the Five Hundred', a people's court, and the people's assembly, the *Ekklesia*.

These controls were intended to protect the people from future tyrants, as was the decision to pay members of courts and councils for attending meetings, so making it possible for the less wealthy to participate in Athenian democracy. This system became the subsequent model for democratic constitutions and was used by Plato and Aristotle in their works on political philosophy. Meanwhile in Sparta control had passed to a succession of successful military leaders in the manner of so many future tyrannies. Typical of this group was King Leonidas, whose stand against the Persians at Thermopylae was to be immortalized. These men were no democrats and maintained a rigid control over their people. Against the interests of the people each devoted much of the national resource to creating and maintaining a powerful army, much as modern dictators in the twentieth century have done.

Even so, many Greeks considered the tyrant not only as their champion in civic matters but also as an occasional necessity in time of war. It was for this reason that a tyrant sometimes usurped power with the active help and support of the people. Gradually attitudes changed, and as democracy became more effective the tyrant became synonymous with arbitrary, despotic and cruel oppression. The greatest philosophers and historians of this second classical age – Plato, Xenophon and Aristotle – all produced works that questioned the inevitability of the rise of such men. They also sought to define the rights and obligations needed by society to maintain a free people. Each philosopher studied the careers of past tyrants in great detail, comparing them to each other and debating the circumstances of their rise, achievements and fall. According to Plato it was inevitable that the temptations of prosperity must inevitably lead to corruption and that the ruler would become the master of the people rather than their ally. Each tyrant would begin plotting against the other. What the Greek philosophers also predicted was that tyrants, in addition to controlling individual liberties, would need to suppress public opinion in order to maintain their power. Or as the first emperor of China, Qin Shi Huang, openly stated a century after Aristotle, 'The way to organize a country well is to have no free speech . . . therefore one does not rely on intelligent and thoughtful men. The ruler makes the people single-minded and therefore they will not scheme for selfish profit.' These warnings from the ancient world would certainly come to apply to all future despotisms. What the Greeks also predicted was that the tyrant could never be a contented man, for power does not equate happiness. Plato gives a powerful description of the miserable life of a typical tyrant, 'hemmed in by a ring of warders, all of them his enemies' and racked by fear of and loathing for his subjects. Such a man has the existence of a near-recluse and is unable to enjoy the simple pleasures of the world. He is compelled to bribe and flatter the worst of men, thinking himself rich in worldly possessions but in reality a moral pauper. These views were shared by the great majority of Plato's Athenian contemporaries and produced an acute awareness of the need to preserve the freedom of the people.

For the 'people' the dilemma has always been how to identify these potential tyrants before they acquire total power and subjugate society to their will. One indicator is the eccentricities of their behaviour that can often be inconsistent. Once in power the tyrant is hard to shift because of the ruthlessness with which he is prepared to defend his position. It was a question that obsessed Ancient Greek society and led to an attempt by

Athenian democracy to free itself of potential or actual tyranny by the practice of ostracism. The name is derived from the *ostraka* or broken pottery shards used as voting tokens in the Assembly. Each year the members were offered an ostracism and could name anyone they considered a threat to Athenian democracy. If they approved it, an ostracism was held and citizens gave the name of the person they wished to be ostracized. This was then scratched on a shard and deposited in an urn. Ostracism was crucially different from Athenian law at the time, for there was no charge, and no defence to it could be mounted by the person expelled. Anyone named was automatically found guilty. Although there was no appeal for anyone ostracized, the penalty was relatively mild in comparison to the kind of sentences inflicted by the courts on politicians found to be acting against the interests of the people. In these cases Athenian juries could inflict severe penalties such as death, huge fines, confiscation of property, permanent exile and loss of citizens' rights.

Warnings of the need for the people to guard against the rise of a tyrant passed, like so much else, from the Greeks to the Romans – and with it consideration of the need to recognize the early warning signs. Once a tyrant had seized power he would refuse to relinquish it and the people would have lost control of their own society; from then on there would be only one law in force and this would based solely on the tyrant's will. The problem was to identify the potential tyrant, for, although there are always exceptions to the stereotype, these men could be disarmingly charming and charismatic. Once in power they show a complete lack of self-doubt, unusual self-confidence and an independence of thought and behaviour. They were also convincing liars, without compassion, often sadistic and possessed of a boundless appetite for power.

These are the same character traits that have been clinically diagnosed in the average psychopath. Not surprisingly, many psychologists and historians have suggested that the tyrant and the psychopath are one and the same. According to Canadian psychologist Stephen Hart, psychopaths and tyrants share a compulsion to manipulate people and to use violence and intimidation to gain control over others. Often such individuals are intelligent and charismatic, but the one defining characteristic they have in common is a chronic inability to feel guilt for their actions. As a result the tyrant/psychopath is incapable of remorse and is quite happy to commit vast numbers to prison camps or to summary execution.

A question that intrigued the ancient world was whether being a tyrant was innate or whether such a person could be made by the circumstances of his early life. We now know that the latter is probably true: a tyrant can be produced by such traumatic family experiences as being bullied by his father when a child. This unhappy experience was shared by the two greatest tyrants of the twentieth century: Hitler and Stalin were almost certainly produced in this way. A more recent example, among many others, was the miserable and brutalized childhood that resulted in the adult Saddam Hussein.

Psychologists such as the Swiss expert Alice Miller have argued that a traumatic childhood is the greatest single factor contributing to the making of a tyrant. She suggests that children who have suffered severe abuse at the hands of their fathers become helpless victims of the situation because they are too small and powerless to defend themselves. Permanent damage is done by the shame and humiliation they have to endure. If parental authority is experienced as punishment a child will come to believe, as despots have seemingly always done, that it is 'normal' for power to be used in a repressive, negative and punitive manner. The unconscious conviction is that love and cruelty are one and the same thing, so leading in later life to sadism, which manifests itself in vicious aggression towards any person or group seen as threatening or opposing the tyrant's will. This in turn deeply affects the tyrant's character in adulthood and drives a bitter determination for revenge and a quest for power. This makes the real enemy of the tyrant his cruel or neglectful parent, but the substitute and symbolical target becomes one or more scapegoat groups within his society. What he had endured as a child was a cruel and unfair abuse of adult power without any compensatory experience of respect and affection. He developed an addiction to power and a desire to exert control over the unfortunate society he ruled – just as his persecutors had once exercised control over them.

The cruelties shown by the Roman emperors Caligula and Nero can be seen as the result of such childhood humiliation and deprivation, which provoked later acts of despotic sadism. Caligula, whose very name has become synonymous with irrational cruelty, grew up in an atmosphere of danger and insecurity. Virtually imprisoned on the Isle of Capri by Emperor Tiberius, he was subject to the tyrant's whims and could have at any moment suffered a similar fate to the rest of his late family. This experience certainly contributed to Caligula's brutal and vengeful actions when he became emperor himself. Nor was Caligula's experience unique at the time. His nephew Nero suffered a similar childhood trauma, and one of his earliest child-hood memories was of being torn screaming by soldiers from his mother's arms as she was dragged away and sent off alone into exile and disgrace.

This kind of insecure and brutalized childhood seems to have been experienced by many later tyrants, too, and is the key to understanding their behaviour. In the case of some societies, such as nineteenth-century Germany, this particular form of abuse appears to have been endemic. At the time Adolf Hitler was growing up children were treated harshly as part of German educational policy. They were often denied the love and affection that was considered natural in other societies. As a result an entire generation of potential sociopaths was produced – as is confirmed by the tens of thousands of recorded cases of emotionally maladjusted children. Hitler was just one of them. His subsequent career clearly illustrates the theory of delayed revenge after a damaged childhood. The catalyst was his father, Alois, who subjected young Adolf and his mother to almost daily drunken beatings. Alice Miller believes that it was history repeating itself and that Alois was simply repeating the abuse that he had himself suffered as a child. This was an unconscious attempt to regain the power he had lost in childhood to his own father. As she puts it, 'To beat one's child is to avoid beating oneself. Therefore beating, whether psychological beating or actual beating . . . is a never-ending task.' Sometimes maternal love is a compensation, but in Hitler's case his mother Karla did not appear to show that love that might have compensated for his father's hostility. There may have been millions of Alois Hitlers throughout Germany at the end of the nineteenth century, tyrannizing their sons into a vengeful generation that would easily be recruited by Nazism. Hitler's appalling revenge was to make the Jews the substitute group for childhood abuse and to attempt to wipe out the entire Jewish population both of Germany and the occupied countries of Eastern Europe. It could also be said that not having a son of his own to beat Hitler was symbolically beating an entire race.

A very similar childhood trauma was experienced by that other great tyrant of the twentieth century, Joseph Stalin. He grew up in a small Georgian town with a drunken stepfather who humiliated him by beating him in the presence of an ineffectual mother. As in Hitler's case there was no one to protect him, and his hatred of his father became so intense that in 1906 he attempted to hire an axe man to kill him. Benito Mussolini also suffered as a child and lamented his schooldays. Another twentieth-century tyrant, Mao Tse-tung, also suffered a brutish childhood; but what appeared to have outraged Mao far more than the violence was his father's lack of charity to the poor, which may well have sparked his own concern for the poverty of rural China and caused him to develop a lifelong resentment of his father. The childhood humiliation experienced by other despots was also present in Mao's case, albeit in a milder form: his father used him as a debt collector, sending him round the local village to collect money for the chickens and eggs he had sold. The future ruler of China found this demeaning and embarrassing but not as damaging as his father's insistence that he receive only a minimal education – appropriate to a man who would spend the rest of his life working in the fields. Such treatment provoked anger and contempt in the child. 'I learned to hate him,' Mao later told the American journalist Edgar Snow. But unlike Hitler and Stalin Mao had been able to strike back at his despotic father by persuading the whole family to stand up against him and present a united front. This ability to organize would serve him well in his political career. Throughout his life, Mao constantly referred to how this childhood battle with his father had influenced his later actions.

This, according to Alice Miller, was quite understandable. A child who has experienced parental authority as frustrating and debilitating will, as an adult, use authority in punitive and retaliatory acts. A political despot will use it to enslave a whole society to his will. In this sense power is a poison that eventually overwhelms even an idealist such as Mao. Predictably Mao and the other despots of recent times did not relate to individuals in an empathetic way. Their concern was not with the single person but with the people as a whole. They were convinced that everything they did was for the benefit of the masses in their society. They looked to 'the people' in a tribal or abstract sense – Hitler constant identified with the people in a pan-Germanic sense, while Stalin had a semi-mystical concept of pan-Slavism.

Whatever the causes that make a tyrant there remains the problem of what to do about him once he is in power. Is society justified in assassinating such a man, is murder justified by the public good? It was a question that troubled the Athenians as they sought to protect their democracy. The philosopher Plato was much concerned with the issue. He saw rulers as being suspended in a constant flux of pleasure and pain, with tyrants wallowing in the most pernicious forms of these conditions – such as greed and lust. Agreeing with Socrates and Aristotle, Plato saw tyranny as an errant condition of the soul and asserted that the soul of the tyrant had been corrupted, when he became a slave to passion and gave in to the temptation to profit from injustice. Tyrannicide for Plato was therefore a natural means to correct the anomaly, and a tyrant should automatically forfeit his life. It was appropriate that one of the first genuine tyrannicides in Athenian history was that of Clearchus, tyrant of Heraclea, who was assassinated in 353 BC by two of Plato's pupils. The Greek justification of tyrannicide became part of Roman legal philosophy, too: the Romans considered that to live under tyranny was analogous to existing under slavery. This led to the most famous assassination of the period, that of Julius Caesar in March 44 BC when the conspirators claimed they were restoring republican liberties by doing away with a despotic usurper. More support for such tyrannicide was found in the writings of the staunch republican Cicero. He argued that the act was justified on the basis of the principles of natural law.

With the coming of Christianity attitudes changed, partly influenced by Saint Augustine who adamantly rejected such killings as a right and claimed that nobody may arbitrarily kill a fellow man, not even a condemned criminal. Thomas Aquinas, however, contradicted Augustine by suggesting a limited acceptance of tyrannicide. At the time of the Reformation it was Calvin's validation of the right of constitutionally enacted bodies to resist monarchical encroachment that led later Calvinist and Puritan thinkers to come out in favour of tyrannicide. John Knox took it a step further by clearly stating that it was the duty and the right of the people to eliminate a tyrannical ruler, particularly if the ruler stood in the way of the 'true' religion. But this was the age of divine absolutism. It was widely accepted that tyrannicide violated the supposed bond between the deity and the monarch. The purported tyrannicide of King Charles I of England was a classic example of this. Condemned by many, it was vigorously defended by the poet John Milton who hailed tyrannicide as not only lawful but laudable and defended the right of the people to execute a tyrant if the established watchdogs failed to manage him effectively.

It was the eighteenth-century philosopher Jean-Jacques Rousseau who arguably provided the most influential account of the Enlightenment concept of tyrannicide. For him citizen and sovereign or ruler were bound together in a social contract and in accordance with the 'general will'. If this bond was broken by a tyrant his violent removal or even assassination was justified. John Locke agreed with Rousseau's conclusion and held the tyrant to be guilty of the greatest crime of all, describing tyranny as the exercise of power beyond right and the tyrant as one in authority who exceeds the power given by the law and who rules for his 'own private, separate advantage'. Yet the problem still remains of finding the correct and just mechanism that decides if and when a tyrant has broken his contract with the people. Any law permitting tyrannicide requires some type of institution to administer it – such as an independent judiciary or tribunal. Only such a valid body is able to assess the alleged tyrannical regime and the conditions under which an act of tyrannicide would be justified and by whom. The practical problem of doing this has faced every modern liberal state and was demonstrated in the 1930s when the German Weimer Republic was unable to protect its civil rights during the onset of Nazism.

2
THE RELIANCE ON APPEARANCE

It could be said that there is no room for real style in a democracy because politicians have to present themselves as self-denying individuals who are devoted to values other than personal vanity. This was certainly not true of Muammar Gaddafi who in the latter years of his reign looked nothing like contemporary democrats or tyrants in their sober suits and military uniforms. What a contrast to the younger Gaddafi who came to power in 1969. Gaddafi soon showed that he preferred a look that was as inconsistent as it was bizarre by constantly appearing in a theatrical wardrobe that seemed to change by the week. His change of image was consistent and continuous as he evolved like some strange butterfly on the world stage. Nature obliged him in this transformation by providing him with reasonable height, an imposing manner and a rubbery clown's face, capable of the most emphatic facial expressions; the seemingly bottomless wardrobe of pantomime costumes he added himself. Whether the look was military simplicity or theatrical finery, no one could match the sheer bravado of Gaddafi of Libya. Although past tyrants often used flamboyant clothes to project an image of wealth, power and superiority, Gaddafi's grandiose display outdid them all. When in vibrantly coloured traditional dress he affected the well-off 'man of the people' look. In military garb he presented himself as 'strong man of the Arab world', able to exert his will over the whole region. When in Western – if eccentric – garb Gaddafi presented himself as an independently minded world statesman with pretensions of influencing the great powers of the globe.

How different it was when he seized power in 1969. The then Colonel Gaddafi stood in simple army uniform at an army parade next to the established strong men of the Arab world, Anwar Sadat of Egypt and Hafez al-Assad of Syria. At that time he was the newcomer and content to show that he was a secular and revolutionary officer as well as being a young rebel. But his wardrobe evolved over the following forty-two years into a bewildering variety of outfits that were carefully chosen for every public occasion and appeared to match his idiosyncratic interpretation of world events. Gaddafi was most often seen sporting long, flowing brown robes that represent his home town of Sirte, a Bedouin town on the Libyan coast. For African summits the self-styled 'king of kings' of Africa donned elaborately decorated dashikis. In the 1980s, at the time of the Lockerbie bombing, he appeared to show his support for world terrorism by wearing a suit and a black shirt and looking like a Libyan version of an Italian Mafioso. By 2009, at the time of the G8 summit, Gaddafi had decided that he needed a sartorial makeover if he wished to be taken seriously as a mainstream international leader. He altered his wardrobe accordingly and began appearing like other world leaders in a far more conventional politician's garb of a plain-cut suit. True, the suit was a startling white and worn without a tie to preserve the wearer's maverick identity. By that time the suit-and-tie formula had become the customary wear for international leaders from China to the USA. Even some heads of state from the Maghreb and the Middle East had begun wearing them – including Saddam Hussein, Hosni Mubarak of Egypt and Ben Ali of Tunisia. Gaddafi did not remain conservatively dressed for long, however. His volatile nature meant that he always retained a compulsion to look different from others. Sometimes he returned to the full-on military dictator look, complete with epaulets and beret. All this culminated in his *pièce de résistance* – a multi-layered, milk-chocolate-coloured satin outfit complete with black beret and a pin in the silhouette of Africa that he wore when he made his first speech to the UN General Assembly on 23 September 2009.

There was also a deeper purpose to Gaddafi's bewildering

array of styles. His clothes and colours were a means of political propaganda and referred, for example, to black Africa and the Arab world. Many of the outfits bore a close resemblance to those that African kings traditionally wore, and Islamic green was prominently featured. His facial expressions, too, were odd. Carefully contrived to look powerful and all-conquering, they in fact often looked merely fatuous. Throughout Gaddafi's long reign in Libya his clothes fascinated the world's journalists and psychologists. The French anthropologist Gilbert Durand suggested that tyrants can be distinguished by the three categories of outfits that they wear: mystical, heroic or synthetic. In Gaddafi's case it was clearly the heroic that he had chosen. Durand also warned that among those who favour the heroic look are many schizophrenic and paranoid personalities who constantly feel persecuted. It was ironic that this peacock of the international stage should suffer such a squalid death in October 2011. Dressed in rags, he was dragged from his hiding place in an underground pipe in the Libyan desert, beaten, abused, stabbed in the anus with a bayonet and finally shot. A more inappropriate end for the flamboyant Muammar Gaddafi is hard to imagine. Strangely the death of an earlier extrovert dictator echoed that of Gaddafi: Benito Mussolini met an equally sordid end and after being shot in April 1945 was taken to Milan and hung upside down at a petrol station.

Appearance had also been important to the Roman emperors centuries earlier. Public display as an indicator of one's position in society was an extremely important feature of Roman life. A man's status and rank was revealed by his dress and would have been immediately apparent to those around him. In particular the clothes worn by a Roman emperor, especially on state occasions, had to be the most sumptuous and made from the rarest and finest materials. No one was more aware of this than Emperor Augustus who even introduced laws regulating exactly what each section of society should wear to attend public spectacles. Those of high rank who appeared without a toga were relegated to the very back rows of the assembly or stadium. This was an essential part of Augustus' determination, according to Suetonius, to make Roman patricians wear the toga on important public occasions and whenever they entered the Forum. Distinctions of dress were also imposed on others of more humble rank to satisfy Augustus' concern. He insisted that the president of the Roman games should wear the toga *picta*, a triumphal dress of a purple and gold worn over a tunic with palm branch designs. Every rank and position in society was now carefully regulated by Augustus' almost fetishistic obsession. Current and past *curule* magistrates such as consuls, praetors and *curule aediles* were ordered to wear the purple-bordered toga, while the rest of the senate were to appear in the simple white toga with a broad purple striped tunic; the equestrians wore a tunic with narrow stripes.

Throughout his reign Augustus was acutely aware that his appearance played an important role in projecting his image to the people and in consolidating his regime as a dynamic replacement for the past republic. Statues of him, almost replicas of the one of him found at the Villa of Livia at Prima Porta near Rome, were almost as common as those of the late Saparmurat Niyazov of Turkmenistan. The statues of Augustus showed him as an idealized figure, a Greek god of the new age; the same image appeared on a new edition of the Roman currency in his era. His influence was applied to all the arts and particularly architecture, and it was said that during his reign Rome was transformed from a mean city of brick to a marvellous city of marble.

Augustus' concern with appearance would certainly have appealed to Benito Mussolini in the twentieth century. Mussolini presided over a fascist regime that in many ways attempted to recreate the glories of Ancient Rome. In his performance as a declamatory orator Il Duce was more like Colonel Gaddafi than the Emperor Augustus; yet if ever a nation needed a leader with a dramatic appearance to match a programme of radical action then it was Italy in the 1930s. On coming to power in 1922 Mussolini established himself as the dominant, most-talked-about political figure in Italy. The way he chose to do it was through public performance and his own personal appearance. From the start his gift for display was demonstrated in the famous March on Rome in October 1922. That event and the publicity surrounding it attracted fascist disciples from all over Italy and made it inevitable that he would be given the role of Italian prime minister.

Mussolini came well equipped for the role he was to play as supreme ruler of a fascist nation. He had been a journalist and in that career had shown a genius for self-promotion. He had often made himself the subject of the articles that he had written when editor of the Milan newspaper *Il Popolo d'Italia*. He had all the skills required as a demagogue, including a convincing and per-suasive manner that appealed to unsophisticated people. In many ways he became the role model for all subsequent dictators of the twentieth century. Aware of the devotion traditionally shown by the Italian peasant people to the birthplace of saints such as St Francis of Assisi, he encouraged his own birthplace at Predappio to become a secular shrine. Crowds of the fascist faithful travelled there, treating it as a kind of modern Bethlehem. Mussolini was also acutely aware of the importance of presentation to the people, having studied books on psychology; he was particularly influenced by Gustav Le Bon's book on the behaviour of crowds. This research was now put to good use: it soon became obvious that Il Duce was a master of oratory and crowd manipulation. His careful self-promotion certainly showed the way forward for Adolf Hitler and, later, Mao Tse-tung.

Mussolini started with the significant advantage of being Italian and therefore heir to the great Roman imperial tradition. The historic stiff-armed Roman salute became the most recognizable gesture of his new fascist regime and the symbol of the *fasces* an important visual icon in the creation of a new Italy. Mussolini's intention was to elevate his image from that of an ambitious bourgeois journalist to a latter-day emperor, with all the qualities of a secular messiah. It was this fusion of Roman history with Roman Catholicism that gave his personality cult its undoubted appeal at a time of both economic and spiritual depression. Within four years he felt confident enough of his sway over the Italian people to abandon the democratic constitution altogether and seize power as the world's first fascist dictator. In the process he suppressed free speech and introduced a comprehensive system of centralized government that he described as 'totalitarianism'.

At the centre of the presentation of the fascist state was the image of Il Duce himself. His portrait showing his pugnacious expression was displayed everywhere and backed by the songs and music of the new fascism on the move. In addition simple and memorable party slogans were devised such as 'Believe, Obey, Fight' and the ubiquitous 'Mussolini Is Always Right'. These were incessantly blared out on state radio and displayed daily in the Italian newspapers. The weekly illustrated magazines – in particular the *Illustrazione Italiana* – maintained a relentless propaganda barrage that invariably showed the actions of Il Duce in the most positive light: if not Mussolini it would be a story about one or other member of his family. The people were encouraged to think of Il Duce as a modern secular saint with schoolchildren all over Italy reciting a near-blasphemous daily verse that included the words, 'He descended to Rome, on the third day he restored the Italian State. He ascended into high office and is seated on the right hand of our Sovereign.' The Vatican appears to have turned a blind eye to this, perhaps endorsing Pope Pius XI's earlier description of Mussolini as a 'man of Providence'. This tacit endorsement by the Pope gave the Italian people every reason to believe that Il Duce was indeed a godlike figure.

Mussolini's image as a man of action who got things done was further enhanced as stories of him dramatically taming wild horses or restoring the sick to health began to appear in the Italian press. On one occasion he was shown driving through Rome in an open-topped car with a lion cub seated on his lap to demonstrate his astonishing mastery of the animal kingdom. Another story claimed that anyone walking through Rome late at night could look up at his office window in the Palazzo Venezia. There his light would still be burning as Il Duce laboured at his desk in dedication to the Italian people. So persuasive were these stories that some thought, that like Christ, Il Duce could even work miracles. Once when he visited Sicily in June 1923, a dangerous eruption of Mount Etna suddenly began but then mysteriously ceased. Could Mussolini have done this? Even more inexplicable was the sudden ending of the long drought in Libya that coincided with the arrival in Tripoli of Il Duce's aeroplane in March 1937. Naturally it came as no surprise to the Italian people when Mussolini survived four assassination attempts in one year alone, merely suffering a wounded nose.

This near-deification of the man compensated in many ways for Il Duce's constantly expressed admiration for Ancient Rome and his attempt to recreate such an empire in modern Italy with himself as a latter-day Roman emperor. Never an Adonis, this short, heavily built, balding man was nevertheless portrayed as the new national ideal. Thousands of images appeared showing Il Duce in varied poses as he went about transforming his native land with fascist prosperity. Often he was shown working alongside the peasants in the fields and stripped to the waist – as Vladimir Putin would appear seventy years later. In some pictures he was seen labouring heroically to help drain the Pontine Marshes, in others strutting in military uniform or hectoring the crowd from the balcony of some provincial town hall in a manner that would be familiar with successive dictators. The image had to be preserved at all costs, so negative comments about his true age, physical failings or state of health were banned in the media.

Mussolini's surroundings were as important as his personal

appearance. Consequently his office in the Palazzo Venezia in Rome was situated in one of the largest rooms in a city of grand salons. Il Duce sat at one end of this huge space to receive visitors like a king in some great classical drama. It was a presentation device that would be copied by Hitler in his chamber at the Berlin Chancellery. The acknowledged Italian national flair for design was harnessed to the presentation of the fascist regime. Even the graphics used in documents and posters were of the highest calibre. As in a modern advertising campaign, a stylish use of the words 'Viva Il Duce' appeared everywhere and were then abbreviated to the single word 'Dux' or even the single letter 'M'. This simple but powerful message was redolent of the ever-present slogans in George Orwell's *Nineteen Eighty-Four*. As with the image of the tyrannical 'Big Brother' in Orwell's prophetic novel, Mussolini's face loomed everywhere – from public buildings, on street corners and from classroom walls; it even appeared as a decoration on women's clothing. No one could leave their house without seeing Il Duce gazing challengingly down at them. As one writer observed, 'Mussolini's head fixed me with severe eyes. My God! What did I do wrong?' At the height of his power it was 'impossible to find a hidden place, a discreet corner where the severe face of the dictator is not observing you'. Soon the staring eyes of the tyrant, even the avuncular, hooded-eyed gaze of Comrade Stalin, became synonymous with the oppression of the modern despotic regime.

This constant use of Mussolini's image can now be seen as one of the first and the most effective political public relations campaigns of the twentieth century, its success judged not only by the future tyrants that emulated it but by the fact that many contemporary international cultural figures were taken in by it. Even the eminent psychologist Sigmund Freud, a future victim of German Fascism himself, was moved to send Il Duce a copy of his latest book, signed and dedicated to 'a Hero of Culture'. Nor was Freud alone in according the Italian dictator the respect thought due to a great modernizer of one of Europe's most artistically important nations. Mussolini's occasional clownish appearance and his mawkish behaviour seemed not to detract from the interest and tolerance that the world granted him, in the same way as Muammar Gaddafi Mussolini's crimes were often considered mere peccadilloes rather than acts of downright evil. Even his brutal invasion of Abyssinia in 1935 was made more palatable for international consumption by his clownish appearance before his troops. Admiration for this new colossus of politics was not confined to Italy alone. Mussolini was increasingly eulogized in the foreign press, both in Europe and the USA. One of his most enthusiastic admirers, the *New York Herald*, praised him in November 1923 as a man who deserved his place in history and a worthy successor to Garibaldi. Similar comparisons were made in the British press, the London *Daily Telegraph* applauding the British government's strange decision to invest him with the Order of the Bath for his services to politics.

Where the USA was concerned it also helped that the Italian fascist regime could be seen as a new bastion against the menace of international Communism. Whatever his comic opera bluster Il Duce was seen as a far more benign and sympathetic figure than either Lenin or Stalin, the grim tyrants of Soviet Russia. As Will Rogers, the famous American columnist wrote, to his later embarrassment, 'Dictator form of government is the greatest form of government: that is if you have the right Dictator.' The Italian historian Simonetta Falasca-Zamponi recalls the initial enthusiasm for Mussolini. She claims that between 1925 and 1928 more than a hundred articles on Mussolini were published in the US press, compared to a mere fifteen on Joseph Stalin. He was even praised by Winston Churchill, who on a visit to Rome in January 1927 declared that Mussolini was the greatest living legislator, telling the beaming dictator to his face that, 'If I had been an Italian I am sure that I should have been wholeheartedly with you from start to finish in your triumphant struggle against the bestial appetites and passions of Leninism. I will, however, say a word on an international aspect of fascism. Externally, your movement has rendered service to the whole world.'

With Mussolini internationally respected and praised at home, his propaganda machine set out to portray Il Duce as the man of the moment at a time of considerable technological and artistic progress. His supporters claimed that his blundering military adventures in Africa were inspired by the work of Tommaso Marinetti and the other Italian Futurist artists. Marinetti had declared, 'War is beautiful because it enriches a flowering meadow with the fiery orchids of machine guns', and this violent concept of art was presented as the philosophical inspiration for Mussolini's imperial campaigns against poorly armed Africans. It had the effect of presenting Mussolini as a man of his times – as did the consistent attempt to associate him with speed and modern machinery. Fast racing cars were a regular pictorial prop, as was that ultimate symbol of modernity in the 1920s, the aeroplane. Pictures of Il Duce as intrepid aviator filled the newspapers and were often accompanied by dramatic stories of his aerial daring. The courage that these high-speed adventures demanded of a real man was constantly emphasized. One report claimed that during the recent First World War he had bravely refused an anaesthetic when having a bullet removed on the battlefield. In 1926 the fascist propaganda machine issued a decree requiring a newsreel featuring Il Duce in wartime action to be screened before every feature film that was shown in Italian cinemas.

Within a decade Adolf Hitler was able to establish an even more successful personality cult than Mussolini's. Hitler's was so effective that in the early years of his rule he seemed just as popular abroad as he was in his native Germany. Hitler also had the good fortune to arrive on the political scene at a time when the mass media offered new opportunities for communicating with the people. The German press had become more sophisticated.

There was state radio and newsreel opportunities at every German cinema. The message of Adolf Hitler and his promises could now be brought to millions of people throughout Germany. With the Mussolini experience as their guide Hitler's Nazi propagandists were able to create an even more effective personality cult for their master – although this was no easy task, given the unappealing personal appearance with which Joseph Goebbels, minister of public enlightenment and propaganda, and Hans Fritzsche, head of the wireless news department, had to work. Hitler presented a far less prepossessing figure than the squat but physically powerful Benito Mussolini. Up until the age of twenty-five he manifested many of the characteristics that some people now associate with the hippies of the 1960s. He was shiftless; seemed to lack any sense of identity; appeared to have no real sense of direction or ambition; was content to live in filth and squalor; worked only when he had to – and then sporadically; and spent most of his time in romantic dreams of being a great artist. Nevertheless this apparently insignificant and incompetent ne'er-do-well was later able, in the course of a relatively few years, to talk his way into the highest political offices, hoodwink the experienced leaders of the major powers, turn millions of highly civilized people into barbarians, order the extermination of a large segment of the population, build and control the mightiest war machine ever known and plunge the world into history's most devastating war.

The Führer's personal appearance was unimpressive and largely unattractive, as he was below average height with wide hips and short legs. Brown, diseased teeth and dirty fingernails completed the unprepossessing picture. Yet the worst physical problem was Hitler's hollow chest, which meant his uniforms had to be specially padded to compensate. He was such a poor specimen that he would probably not have met the basic physical requirements for joining his own SS Guard. Nor was his physical appearance helped by a poor dress sense that was particularly noticeable in the early days of his rise to power. His dramatic political ambitions contrasted markedly with the provincial clothes he chose to wear. In spite of advice to the contrary he insisted on wearing Bavarian national costume that combined curious lederhosen with a white embroidered shirt and a comic feathered hat. When not dressed as a Bavarian yokel, such as when delivering an important speech at a rally, he appeared in an ordinary blue lounge suit. This clerk-like attire gave him a mundane appearance devoid of the impact and authority that Mussolini always exhibited – but that was before he spoke.

Hitler's voice had a hypnotic tone that combined power with a slight harshness. This has been attributed to the effects of a gas attack he suffered during the First World War. The gas may have slightly damaged his vocal chords, giving him an unusual and compelling tone. Whatever the cause, it was highly effective whenever he spoke in public. Many who later heard him at public rallies claimed that his voice had a hypnotic quality. Yet if his voice was impressive then his walk certainly was not. According to one observer it had a strange mincing almost comical quality. 'It was a very ladylike walk with dainty little steps. Every few steps he would twitch his right shoulder nervously while his left leg jerked up as he did so.' The American journalist Edgar Mowrer watched him in court at the trial that followed the unsuccessful Munich Beer Hall Putsch and was astonished to see the almost total lack of charisma in this strange little man who had caused so much trouble. Mowrer doubted that anyone who looked so insignificant could really be the Messiah that the German people awaited. 'Was this provincial dandy, with his slick dark hair, his cutaway coat, his awkward gestures and glib tongue, the terrible rebel? He seemed for all the world more like a travelling salesman for a clothing firm,' he wrote. Mowrer appears to have missed Hitler's one redeeming physical feature that was frequently mentioned by witnesses – his eyes. These were bright blue bordering on violet and totally mesmeric. Most importantly, like his voice, they were strangely hypnotic and seemed to transfix every member of the audience whenever he spoke. The Canadian prime minister at the time, Mackenzie King, was very impressed by Adolf Hitler and reported admiringly, 'He is really one who truly loves his fellow man and his country . . . his eyes impressed me most of all. There was a liquid quality about them which indicated keen perception and profound sympathy.' The German people were equally impressed. A policeman who had previously disliked Hitler intensely reluctantly attended a Nazi rally and was immediately won over by the man. He found himself gazing at Hitler as he entered the hall. Hitler looked straight back at him with an irresistible stare. 'From that moment, I was lost,' the policeman told his friends. 'The following day I became a National Socialist. Heil Hitler!'

From the 1920s onwards the Nazi Party had targeted German youth as a special audience for Hitler's propaganda and dynamic presentation. They emphasized that the party was a movement of youth, resilient and hopeful for the future. Millions of German young people were thus won over to Nazism in the classroom and through extracurricular activities. In January 1933, the Nazis' youth organization, the Hitler Youth, had 50,000 members, but by the end of the year this figure had increased to more than 2 million. By 1936 membership of the Hitler Youth increased to 5.4 million. In 1939 membership became mandatory. The German authorities then prohibited or dissolved other competing youth organizations such as the Boy Scouts and the Girl Guides.

Nowhere was appearance more important for Hitler and the Nazi regime than at the Nuremberg rallies. These Nazi Party celebrations were held every September from 1923 until 1938. Brilliantly choreographed by Joseph Goebbels, they lasted a week and drew as many as 1 million people to the city from all over Germany. The central events comprised numerous roll calls in the presence of Adolf Hitler as well as mass parades of all-important organizations of the Nazi state. The whole scene was memorably captured in 1933 and 1934 by the filmmaker Leni Riefenstahl who in 1934 used thirty film cameras and 120 technicians to record the events. Featuring striking camera angles and dramatic lighting effects, Riefenstahl's masterpiece, *Triumph of the Will*, far exceeded anything that the fascist regime in Italy had ever produced. Above all it gave a visual credibility to the Nazis that Hitler would ruthlessly exploit in the coming years. In 1934 the rally was attended by the American journalist William L. Shirer, the future historian of the Third Reich, who was impressed by the presentation of the Führer and his impact on the people. He declared that Hitler was 'restoring pageantry and color and mysticism to the drab lives of twentieth-century Germans', adding that 'this morning's opening meeting . . . was more than a gorgeous show; it also had something of the mysticism and religious fervor of an Easter or Christmas Mass in a great Gothic cathedral . . . Hitler appeared in the back of the auditorium and followed by his aides, Göring, Goebbels, Hess, Himmler and the others, he slowly strode down the long center aisle while thirty thousand hands were raised in salute.' To Shirer the atmosphere within the hall had the effect that 'every word dropped by Hitler seemed like an inspired word from on high. Man's – or at least the German's – critical faculty is swept away at such moments, and every lie pronounced is accepted as high truth itself.'

Joseph Goebbels predictably was euphoric when describing Hitler's gift of oratory, 'He has the amazing gift of sensing what is in the air. He has the ability to express things so clearly, logically and directly that listeners are convinced that that is what they have always thought themselves. That is the true secret of the effectiveness of Adolf Hitler's speeches.' The psychological impact on the German people went much deeper. In addressing an audience Hitler needed only to dwell on the longings, ambitions, hopes and desires of his own earlier life to awaken these hidden tendencies in his listeners. He did this with great skill, arousing the same attitudes and emotions in his listeners that he himself experienced. Thus he was able to win them to his new view of life, which set a premium on brutality, ruthlessness, dominance, determination and so on – and which dismissed all the established human qualities. The way ahead, he implied, was to strive to be what you are not and to do your best to exterminate that which you are.

3
MASTERS OF STYLE

I t was the poet Juvenal who first used the phrase *'panem et circenses'*, or 'bread and circuses', to describe the stylish public shows that Roman rulers provided to keep their people entertained. These performances were part of a political strategy used by an often tyrannical regime to head off public discontent and rebellion. On offer were distributions of free food, invitations to public baths, gladiatorial combat and exotic animal contests, chariot races, sport and theatrical shows. It was an efficient if costly way for the emperor to keep the population peaceful and at the same time give them the opportunity to shout and display emotion in an open arena. For more than five hundred years these spectacular events were the most important leisure activities of the masses in all parts of the Roman Empire.

In Rome itself there were frequent public holidays celebrated with magnificent and costly shows while comedies, tragedies, pantomimes and bawdy folk plays were staged in the theatres. The most important venue was the Colosseum, which opened in AD 80. Gladiators fought one other or with wild animals to satisfy the bloodlust of the crowd, while hundreds of thousands of spectators packed the stands of the Circus Maximus to enjoy the thrills of chariot racing. The venues and arenas were funded by political leaders including Pompey or by Augustus' generals such as Titus Statilius Taurus. Some of the events dated back to the funerary rituals of Etruscan and Greek cities. As with the modern Olympics local notables would sponsor the huge costs of the games to public acclaim and their own political benefit. On one occasion the tyrannical Emperor Titus held games that lasted more than a hundred days and in which 10,000 men battled against 3,500 wild animals from Africa. On another occasion his fellow-emperor Trajan celebrated his victory over the Dacians by organizing vast battles on a similar scale. These events were never to be surpassed as they were funded by the 10 million kilograms of gold (11,000 short tons), 20 million kilograms (22,000 short tons) of silver and 500,000 slaves that Trajan had looted from the Dacians. Not surprisingly the emperor appeared in a prominent and very visible position at such public spectacles, and the games were increasingly used to consolidate the power of the reigning emperor. Like the sports stars of today the top gladiators, charioteers and actors became folk heroes, and the power of their universal appeal was exploited by politicians and tyrants alike.

During his youth the future tyrant Julius Caesar was famous for the lavish games that he provided for the people. This fuelled suspicion among his political opponents that he had ambitions to become supreme ruler of Rome by establishing himself as the new and generous friend of the people. In the manner of future dictators he was said to have borrowed vast sums of money to fund these projects. The plan certainly worked, for their success made him a prominent figure in Roman life and led to him being given increasingly important public offices. The revenues from these influential positions then enabled him to repay much of his borrowings. Besides using them as a political strategy Caesar had a true passion for the games. As he had anticipated, the people were grateful to him and showered him with honours and positions. Given much the people began to demand even more, clamouring for even more magnificent entertainments. Eventually as the cost continued to escalate Caesar began to tire of trying to satisfy public demand. He passed the role of impresario to his adopted son Octavian Augustus, who felt compelled to organize even more eye-catching and elaborate events.

When power passed to the Emperor Nero a new era of civic display under a tyrannical ruler began. Nero was a great admirer of all things Greek and deliberately cultivated a charioteer's hairstyle and wore Greek-style or theatrical clothing, a practice that deeply upset the more conservative Roman patricians. The chronicler of Nero's reign, Suetonius, observed the eccentric clothes and behaviour and wrote of Nero's apparent egalitarian attitudes in the early years of his rule, 'He gave many entertainments of different kinds: the Juvenales, chariot races in the Circus, stage-plays and a gladiatorial show.' From the first, 'he even had old men of consular rank and aged matrons take part. For the games in the Circus he assigned places to the knights apart from the rest, and even matched chariots drawn by four camels.' At the plays he gave 'parts were taken by several men and women of both the orders'. 'Every day all kinds of presents were thrown to the people; these included a thousand birds of every kind each day, various kinds of food, tickets for grain, clothing, gold, silver, precious stones, pearls, paintings, slaves, beasts of burden and even trained wild animals; finally, ships, blocks of houses and farms.'

Nero sat watching these events from the top of the proscenium and, remarkably for the times, as Suetonius continues, 'within the space of a single year, he had no one put to death, not even criminals'. Instead 'he compelled four hundred senators and six hundred Roman knights, some of whom were well-to-do and of unblemished reputation, to fight in the arena. Even those who fought with the wild beasts and performed in the arena were from the same orders.' In the arts he was a keen participant himself, accepting the prize 'for Latin oratory and verse, for which all the most eminent men had contended but which was given to him with their unanimous consent'. When the judges offered him the prize for playing the lyre he knelt, in a theatrical gesture, and 'ordered that it be laid at the feet of Augustus' statue'.

Nero also took a great interest in design and architecture. His greatest success was his influence on the coinage design that during his reign became the finest in all Rome's history. In architecture, too, Nero exercised an important influence, becoming the leading patron of his day and encouraging Roman builders to be more adventurous with their designs. During his reign more vaults, domes and arcades appeared, and the new buildings of Rome were significantly taller and grander than those of the past. Unlike his predecessors Nero did not confine his projects to the city of Rome but commissioned many villas and canals in rural areas. Perversely the Great Fire of AD 64, for which he was unfairly blamed, should have provided the opportunity for him to rebuild the city in a more comprehensive and a bolder manner had not public hostility intervened. It also thwarted his even more ambitious plan to extend the city of Rome down to the port of Ostia. His favourite project, however, remained a grandiose new city that would bear his own name. Little of this was built other than a new royal palace for himself. A vast structure occupying more than 50 hectares (120 acres) but built in the style of a country villa, it occupied the summit of the Velia Hill. Magnificently decorated with gold and precious stones it was condemned by Nero's critics. The poet Martial called it 'the hated entrance hall of the cruel king'. After Nero's death it remained an embarrassing monument to imperial extravagance and was swiftly stripped of its valuable materials and left to decay. Painters of the Renaissance preserved its memory by copying many of the innovative visual themes and idiosyncrasies it had pioneered.

Using style to consolidate a regime became a regular practice of later tyrants. One of the most aesthetically successful exponents was Napoleon Bonaparte. After seizing power in France and declaring himself emperor in 1804, Napoleon was particularly successful in helping create a style that gave a distinctive identity to his regime. Indeed the word 'Empire' came to define the dominant style of the age – a comprehensive look ranging from interior design to high fashion. Napoleon, a true meritocrat, was quick to utilize the skills of those around him, not least those of the great painter Jacques-Louis David. Having gained power through his political and military achievements, Napoleon saw the need to legitimize and promote his new regime. Artists, designers and architects were of particular importance, and he appointed Charles Percier and Pierre-François-Léonard Fontaine his official architects and designers. The style they created, which came to characterize the Empire period, relied heavily on militaristic elements that included symbols of war and victory. These were combined with the traditional imperial emblems of Ancient Rome such as the golden eagle and classical palm and laurel wreath motif. Napoleon used this classical imagery to encourage the French people to make a direct visual connection between his regime and the power of the Roman Empire.

Napoleon's Egyptian campaign, although a military failure, proved an aesthetic success. As well as bringing back the Rosetta Stone that enabled linguists to decipher Ancient Egyptian hieroglyphs, it provoked a craze in France for all things Egyptian. The detailed drawings of art and architecture published on his return by artist and archaeologist Dominique-Vivant Denon led to the incorporation of Egyptian motifs in the furniture and decorative arts of the following decades. As well as military emblems, Egyptian and classical imagery, the Empire period also embraced imagery of love, sensuality and seduction. The emperor's personal images comprised the bee, a symbol of immortality and resurrection, specifically chosen by Napoleon to link his new empire to the very origins of France. The initial of the emperor, 'N' for Napoleon, was frequently used, and its success certainly inspired the use of the single letter 'M' by Benito Mussolini almost a century later. Surrounded by the sartorial splendour of his court, Napoleon remained a low-key figure often dressed in a simple military uniform but surrounded by French commanders decked out in martial finery of brilliant colours. This visual modesty was intended to imply that, in spite of his great successes on the battlefield, he remained a simple man of the people.

Yet not even Napoleon could match Benito Mussolini in his dedication to a stylish regime. Every aspect of his fascist state showed how conscious Il Duce was of the need to present the new system in the most attractive way. Attention to detail was his particular forte as his son-in-law Count Ciano revealed in an account of a military parade in 1939. 'He takes personal care of the minutest detail. He spends hours at the window of his office spying on the movements of the troops. He has ordered the bandmaster to use a baton and teaches him in person the right movements.' To Il Duce style was almost as important as content, and this was reflected in every aspect of his new fascist state. He was convinced that if the character of the Italian people was to change then the transformation must begin with a new civic look and new customs. He was also interested in creating arm gestures and salutes that would act as unifying displays for the new state. Such greetings also signalled a complete submission by the individual to the new state.

A new political uniform was created in the form of the fascist blackshirt – the icon of the party, the wearing of which demonstrated an individual's allegiance and loyalty to the state. Mussolini also ordered the Italians to identify the blackshirt with the ethical values of the regime, such as courage and struggle, and insisted that its wearing should be treated with great respect. Rules were introduced to define how and when it could be worn. One requirement was that the sleeves must never be rolled up in a casual manner. Parades for Italian youth were organized on a national scale, the young participants invariably dressed in fascist black and marching along with the Passo Romano, the Italian version of the goose step. Mussolini himself wore the blackshirt only sporadically as part of an ever-changing wardrobe of costumes that reflected his non-stop round of activities – pilot, racing driver, all-round man of action. With the blackshirt Il Duce demonstrated his realization that the stylish presentation of his regime to the people was of vital importance and depended on well-designed simplicity.

So effective was Mussolini's presentation that it became the standard for the more powerful tyrants of the twentieth century. Hitler, Stalin and later Mao Tse-tung followed his style. They kept their appearance less flamboyant, being always careful to be seen and photographed in plain military uniform devoid of flashy medals and decorations and little different from that of an ordinary soldier. Hitler was particularly careful to wear the one simple decoration that he had actually won in the First World War: the Iron Cross, First Class. In Stalin's case it was the badge of a Hero of the Soviet Union. Stalin astutely always kept the look of his regime simple while ruthlessly establishing his own personality cult. This was based on his understanding of Russian history and his perception that the Russian people needed to look up to a single godlike figure. Stalin cleverly presented himself as the current manifestation of this character. In the past it had been the tsar; now it was Joseph Stalin.

Throughout the twentieth century there were many other tyrants, particularly in South America, who followed Mussolini's example by appearing on balconies and addressing the people in full military uniform. As successive nations became repressive tyrannies their leaders returned to the Napoleonic model of colourful uniforms awash with gold braid and medals commemorating battles that had never been fought. More recently, with the arrival of Fidel Castro in Cuba, a more casual look featuring low-key army fatigues became the norm. This was intended to present the tyrant as a true socialist revolutionary and a man of the people. Resplendent or casual, the army uniform underlined the ruler's need to keep his society in a state of tension. The people must be made to feel that their nation was under a constant state of threat from enemies beyond its borders. At its most extreme the people had to be convinced that they were in a state of undeclared war and that anyone who opposed the regime was a traitor and an unpatriotic counter-revolutionary.

A similar attempt to manipulate the people was adopted in

Vietnam, Cambodia and North Korea. In North Korea Kim Jong-il, son of the founder of the regime, caused much amusement among foreign journalists by always appearing in a beige one-piece jumpsuit and a pair of platform shoes. Ignoring the international mockery, the country's state-run newspaper *Rodong Sinmun* praised their 'Dear Leader' claiming implausibly that his jumpsuit had given him to the status of an international fashion icon. The foreign press responded by suggesting that the outfit had a more practical function as a covering disguise for the bulletproof vest that he always wore in case of an attempted assassination. The look of both leader and regime became even gloomier when Kim Jong-il's heir to the control of North Korea, his son Kim Jong-un, came to power in December 2011 and immediately appeared in his own version of the family sartorial look, a long black coat and an improbable hairstyle.

As with the tyrannies of the past, the Kim dynasty were very concerned with creating a state architecture that reflected their control of aesthetics as well as of the people. Kim Jong-il himself shared the fondness of his fellow dictators for symbolic excess, claiming that symbolic gestures provide 'the best visual and lasting means of conveying the leader's achievements and his greatness to posterity'. In 1991 Kim Jong-il wrote *On Architecture*, a 170-page account of the nature and role of architecture in the North Korean state with whole chapters devoted to monumental design and symbolism. Translated into English, it later appeared on the internet, providing an intriguing insight into the peculiar imagination of a tyrant for whom society can be manipulated like a toy building set. Much of the content is stock Marxist–Leninist thinking with such phrases as 'revolutionary outlook', 'party loyalty' and 'decadent reactionary bourgeois' constantly appearing. The rest of the content would not be out of place in any standard architectural textbook.

The central theme is a proposal for 'Juche' architecture, an invention of Kim Jong-il's father, Kim Il-Sung. 'Juche' is

the central idea of the North Korean form of isolationist communism, a combination of self-reliance and national independence. It is designed to meet the supposed aspirations and demands
of the masses – convenience, cosiness, beauty and durability. As a
result Pyongyang, according to Kim, became the most beautiful
city in the world and has been showered with wonderful
monuments. A statue of Kim Il-Sung adorns a hilltop; an Arch of
Triumph straddles a major boulevard; the Tower of the Juche Idea,
resembling the Washington Monument, sits on a central axis. The
most ambitious monumental structure in Pyongyang, however, is
the 105-storey, 330-metre-tall (1,100-foot) Ryugyong Hotel.
Unfinished and abandoned since 1992 this vast pyramid towered
over the city for nearly two decades until work resumed in 2008, an
unwitting icon of failure. Kim Il-Sung's obsessive fascination with
architecture is one that has often been typical of the dictatorial
personality. As architecture promises compensation for the insuf-
ficiencies of worldly power, it offers something concrete to under-
pin and justify the failings of the regime. In the twentieth century
no dictator worth his salt neglected architecture. Hitler was still
tinkering with his model of the new city of Germania even as the
Red Army closed in on Berlin.

Before Saddam Hussein came to power Baghdad in 1958 had
just three public sculptures. Saddam was determined to associate
himself with legendary Islamic figures of the past. He ordered a
statue of himself that depicted him on a white horse, drawing a
clear parallel to Hussein, one of Shi'ite Islam's most revered
figures. He then ordered other works of art that associated him
with Ali, the fourth caliph and the patron saint of Shi'ism. During
the years of the Iran–Iraq war more works appeared that linked
him to Sa'ad ibn Abi Waqqas, an early Arab warrior who brought
Islam to Iran. There were not only monumental sculptures but
kitsch depictions on cheap wall pictures and on the faces of
wristwatches. Like most tyrants Saddam constantly interfered
with the construction of the larger monuments. Perhaps the most

notorious was gigantic Victory Arch in Baghdad. Taller than the Arc de Triomphe in Paris, it depicts two vast forearms with fists holding crossed swords. The architects worked using plaster casts of Saddam's own arms. The huge swords were made from the melted steel taken from the weapons of Iraqi soldiers who had been killed on the battlefield in the Iran war. Five thousand Iranian helmets gathered off the battlefield complete the monument. Chillingly Saddam's monuments often foreshadowed the future rather than just commemorating the past. He ordered construction of the Martyr's Monument just seven months into the Iran–Iraq war even before there were many martyrs to glorify. He then ordered work on the Victory Arch three years and tens of thousands of deaths before the end of the Iran–Iraq war. As in Shelley's poem 'Ozymandias' most of the palaces and grotesque monuments on the banks of the Tigris were reduced to ruins after the US invasion.

Even Saddam's compulsion to present himself and his regime in an heroic light pales before that of President Saparmurat Niyazov of Turkmenistan. Between 1985 and 2006 he bombarded his people with so many narcissistic images of himself that it would have been difficult for any of his fellow citizens to escape depictions of him anywhere in Turkmenistan. He was there in almost every open space in every town; scarcely a public space did not get a statue of the Turkmenbashi, as he was known, placed in a prominent position. Like Mussolini before him, Niyazov beamed down from the walls of workshops and school classrooms and appeared in hotel foyers, adorned bank notes and was even seen on vodka bottle labels. His image was as ubiquitous as that of Christ in a Roman Catholic country. To heighten the impact of the great man many statues were embellished with gold paint and he was always shown symbolically facing east towards the rising sun. The tallest of them stood at the very centre of the capital city Ashgabat, perched on a mechanical stand that slowly rotated to follow the sun. Even in the ancient world there had never been such a display of self-adulation. All this Niyazov considered completely appropriate for a man who had done so much for his country, 'If I was a worker and my president gave me all the things they have here in Turkmenistan, I would not only paint his picture I would have his picture on my shoulder or on my clothing,' Niyazov proudly claimed.

The Turkmenbashi's rise to power was typical of many a modern tyrant. By chance he was perfectly placed as head of the local Communist Party when Soviet rule collapsed in Turkmenistan in 1991. Seizing power with the help of the army he set about establishing a ruthless and all-embracing personality cult. The inspiration for his narcissistic cult had come to him as early as 1979 during a visit to Kim Il-Song in North Korea. There he had been impressed by the way in which Kim had established his own military and intellectual control over the people. When he came to power himself, Niyazov was determined to do the same in Turkmenistan. Yet he took it one step further, and, ignoring the fact that his was an Islamic country, he proclaimed himself the new spiritual as well as the political leader of the people. His thoughts and writing, he told the people, would rival those of the Prophet himself. In 2004 he further consolidated his position by ordering that sections from his own philosophical treatise, the *Rukhnama* or Book of the Soul, be inscribed alongside verses from the Koran. At the same time work began on a new $100-million mosque in his home village just outside Ashgabat. To minimize competition from the Prophet himself Niyazov forbade the construction of any new mosques in the whole of Turkmenistan. Those mosques already standing and all Christian churches were required to display a copy of the *Rukhnama* alongside the Bible or the Koran. Every evening at dusk a new page of the bulky volume had to be turned to reveal further wisdom. The *Rukhnama* was now the source of all wisdom, and every teacher or university student was selected solely on the basis of knowledge of the *Rukhnama*.

Other tyrants to the west, in central Europe, were using different forms of display for self-promotion – among them sporting contests. During this era sport provided templates of competition and combat in the Soviet Union under Stalin and in East Germany. Sporting competition with the rest of the world became almost an alternative to outright war. Eastern Bloc sportsmen and women were the soldiers of communism expected to inflict regular defeat on competitors from the degenerate West.

It was not until the advent of Stalin that the far-reaching possibilities of sport as a means of influencing and controlling the young were fully appreciated. He was the first dictator to discover the value of sport; others merely seized upon the idea and broadened it. 'Every citizen', said Stalin, 'has a duty to be physically fit and ready to repulse any attack from outside.' He had no deep interest in sport as such but saw it as a training routine for physical health. He was interested in athletics for the masses because the soldiery of the nation comes from the masses and a physically fit nation means a fit army. In 1930 Stalin signed a decree organizing physical education throughout all Soviet Russia. Private sporting clubs and organizations were abolished, and athletics of every kind was placed in the hands of the state. He arranged the general scheme of sport in Russia that Mussolini had adapted. To keep the young Italian people occupied and hence contented Mussolini, from the beginning, appreciated the importance of athletics. With the Soviet example before him he saw early on that sport could be used to militarize the nation; he also saw that it was possible to go further than Soviet Russia had gone. The tyrannies and dic-tatorships of the twentieth century came to rank sport alongside traditional propaganda such as historical re-enactments and massive open-air spectacles. Sport helped to instil military-style discipline and orderliness. Historically this was nothing new – merely a return to the practice in Ancient Greece when dictatorial regimes allocated an important role to sport and stylish display to sustain and popularize the state.

4
A NARCISSISTIC PERSONALITY CULT

What every tyrant has had in common is the unshakeable conviction of his own uniqueness and importance. Along with this egotism is the expectation that others must automatically follow him wherever he chooses to lead. Apart from a total lack of self-doubt the tyrant has an almost total inability to recognize the feelings, needs and the viewpoints of others. The catalogue continues – the tyrant has a tendency to misrepresent facts and to ignore any data that conflicts with his own fantasy world and the need to maintain control at all times. Given this package of psychological liabilities it is not surprising that tyrannical leaders are incapable of seeing themselves and their relationships to others realistically. They begin to see the world around them in simpler, automatic ways. According to the psychologist Renana Brooks, the late Saddam Hussein was a typical example of such a personality. Convinced of his power and capacity to dominate, he refused to stop lying about whether or not he had weapons of mass destruction even as bombers prepared to attack Baghdad. 'Dictators are willing to create a fantasy of their personal power,' wrote Brooks; 'they see themselves as heroic, and when that sense of heroism is challenged they become paranoid.'

It seems that not all tyrants have suffered this failure to listen to others from the moment they achieve power; some become seduced by power over time. An example of this pernicious change is Robert Mugabe of Zimbabwe. As a younger man he was apparently a reasonable and a careful listener to the advice of those around him. But as the years passed the seduction of power grew and he became ever more despotic in manner: he seldom bothered with the advice of his colleagues, now convinced of his own infallibility. Mugabe, like past tyrants, had developed an unshakeable belief in his own opinions and was convinced that he was a messianic figure sent to lead his people out of colonial subjugation. In this he was repeating the folly of such past tyrants as Hitler and Stalin and more recently Ayatollah Khomeini of Iran. They all suffered from what the American psychiatrist Jerrold Post has referred to as 'malignant narcissism'. These narcissistic rulers see themselves as the unique saviours of their people and are able, when things inevitably start to go wrong, to blame the mistakes on outside forces. These forces may be the opposition or a group within their country whose members are condemned to become the scapegoats. As such they must be unmasked and rooted out. In Hitler's case the chosen group was the Jews. In an interview given soon after he came to power Hitler admitted that if the Jew did not exist he would have needed to invent him in order to unite the German people. A member of a Japanese delegation visiting Nazi Germany at the time lamented, 'I wish we had something like this in Japan, but we don't because we haven't any Jews.' Other tyrannical regimes were more fortunate than the Japanese in having a ready-made minority group that was available for persecution.

With a lack of empathy or understanding of others goes the tyrant's narcissistic compulsion to promote himself to the people. There was no better exponent of this, as has been shown, than President Saparmurat Niyazov of Turkmenistan. The adulation that he sought was completely appropriate in his opinion for a man who had done so much for his country. Niyazov was the ultimate control freak – personally deciding almost everything that happened in Turkmenistan, including who entered, who left the country, who got into university and who did not. There was no press freedom in Turkmenistan, and all media was under his personal control. When referring to the president newspapers and television were told to use approved phrases such as 'the guarantor of the nation's progress and independence' and 'visionary architect of the nation's future'. Niyazov even rewrote the calendar and renamed the month of January 'Turkmenbashi' with April named after his mother. Behind the bombast there was the usual exploitation and tyranny. Niyazov was accused of siphoning off most of the country's estimated $2 billion a year in gas revenues and concealing them in offshore accounts. He also made sure that any opposition was crushed. Any criticism or dissent was defined as treason and was punishable by long prison terms, confinement to a psychiatric hospital or internal banishment to the arid salt flats on the shores of the Caspian Sea. Informers were encouraged in the customary tyrannical manner and phone calls and e-mails monitored. When Niyazov died suddenly in 2006 the nation could scarcely cope, as the whole infrastructure had depended on the almost total control of one man.

A visit to North Korea was the inspiration for the narcissistic personality cult of another tyrannical regime similar to that of Saparmurat Niyazov. The husband and wife team of Nicolae and Elena Ceauşescu formed their unusual married-couple personality cult in Romania after a visit to North Korea in 1971. Coming from the chaotic and ramshackle Romania of the early 1970s, they were impressed by the organized society they found in Pyongyang. Although communist in character, it had retained its own identity with a national commitment to hard work and zero tolerance of any political dissent. Above all they were intrigued by the highly successful personality cult that Kim Il-Sung had established there. On returning to Bucharest they set about establishing a similar one of their own. The Romanian propaganda machine was then ordered to present Nicolae Ceauşescu as the main architect of both domestic and foreign policies, a visionary and the guarantor of a Romanian path to socialism. Soon pictures of both Ceauşescus began appearing throughout the country and the state media began devoting hours of radio and television time to accounts of their doings. Ceauşescu himself was increasingly portrayed by the Romanian media as a creative communist theoretician and political leader whose 'thought' was the source of all national accomplishments. The time of his presidency was to be known as the 'golden era of Nicolae Ceaușescu'. The media embellished all references to him with standard phrases that referred to him as the nation's guardian and visionary guide to the future. In 1989 Ceaușescu was not only head of state but also headed the Communist Party and the armed forces as well as being chairman of the Supreme Council for Economic and Social Development, president of the National Council of Working People and chairman of the Socialist Democracy and Unity Front.

One curious aspect of the Ceaușescu dictatorship was the competitive nature of the relationship between husband and wife tyrant. While Elena craved international recognition as a scientist, Nicolae sought world approval as a gifted statesman – although neither had the specific abilities required. To advance their particular causes they ordered Romanian ambassadors abroad to lobby foreign media on their behalf. In Nicolae's case this proved a fiasco when an Italian journal that praised him as 'one of the world's greatest leaders and thinkers' proved to be a small language school in Naples run by an old lady. He had better luck with the British government whose foreign minister David Owen described him as 'a statesman of worldwide repute, experience and influence'. Elena meanwhile played a full part in the tyrannical double act, insisting that she be involved in any negotiations with visiting foreign diplomats. She also made herself the official Communist Party boss of Romania and insisted that her birthday be made a national holiday. In the twentieth century only Eva Peron in Argentina ever came so close as Elena Ceaușescu to exercising dictatorial power as a woman. Unfortunately she displayed a cold, unfeeling character and showed affection for no one but her husband and, like Hitler, her dogs. As one former minister described her, 'She was totally negative. She was mean; she always had to have her own way. She was Ceaușescu's devil. As with a mentally unstable character, you tried to avoid her. He [Nicolae] was someone you could talk to, he had a human touch, but she was unadulterated evil.' Both Ceaușescus were obsessed with material possessions, and the gifts they received from foreign dignitaries were shown on television to stress their supposed importance and that of Romania in international affairs.

The inevitable consequence of any personality cult is that the subject comes to believe implicitly in his or her own myth. In the Ceaușescus' case, this overwhelmed their native common sense, resulting in delusions of grandeur that earned them international ridicule. Elena made herself head of both the National Council on Science and the Council on Technology even though she did not possess the capability of producing a scientific paper – thus proving her Ph.D to be a fraud. In spite of this failing her main obsession became the acquisition of honorary science degrees from foreign universities. These she collected with such mania that the bestowing of such honours became the prerequisite for any state visit abroad. As one Romanian journalist commented, 'Being an ignorant, uneducated, primitive kind of woman, she really thought that if she had titles after her name it would change her image.' The Romanian department of foreign affairs had specific orders to negotiate with prominent institutions in whatever country the Ceaușescus were to visit to acquire honorary rewards for Elena, or else the couple would not accept the invitation for a state visit. In advance of a visit to Britain in 1978 she lobbied desperately for an award from either Oxford or Cambridge but had to settle for a far more modest honour from Central London Polytechnic. Before Elena and Nicolae Ceaușescu went on to visit the USA she was told that President Carter could not assure her an honorary degree from a Washington-based institute; Elena muttered vehemently, 'Come off it! You can't sell me the idea that Mr Peanut [Carter] can give me an Illwhatsis diploma but not any from Washington.' However, as no other US university acknowledged Elena's scientific achievements, she had to give in and accept the honorary degree that was being offered. She showed her abhorrence at having to accept this 'low-ranked' degree and on top of it from the hands of a 'dirty Jew' – Dr Emanuel Merdinger, who was the head of the Illinois Academy of Science. Nicolae, too, was obsessed with his own self-importance, once storming out of a dinner in the USA because a Roman Catholic cardinal had dared to say a Christian grace before the meal; a few days later he did the same again, when the mayor of New York dared to suggest that the Romanian people were being denied freedom of worship. This petulant behaviour proved counter-productive for Nicolae's international credibility. In Bucharest the physical symbol of their joint personality cult was the enormous Spring Palace under construction in the centre of Bucharest. Grotesquely over-ornate it was mocked as a bad-taste version of the Palace of Versailles.

There is little doubt that Nicolae Ceauşescu in particular was well aware that it was the Christian religion with its powerful imagery that had sustained the Romanian people during the long years of Turkish oppression. As his unpopularity grew, he attempted to use Christianity to sustain his own personality cult. Romania was presented with a new communist Holy Trinity, himself at the head and Elena and the people making up the triumvirate. Government-controlled media were ordered to play along and began using such phrases as 'the saviour', 'the sacred word' and the 'unifying nimbus' to indicate divine approval for Ceauşescu's actions. One poem composed in his honour even paraphrased the Nicene Creed with the words, 'Man will return to Eden and the Ceauşescu Era will have no end.' These words were designed to be learned and repeated in the manner of traditional Christian litany. Even the Romanian intelligentsia wilted beneath the power of the personality cult and began vying with each other in praise of the great man in the hope of gaining favour with him or his wife. The

Romanian historian Dan Berindel later admitted that he had joined this group for recognition and in return for a government flat in Bucharest. He was prepared to quote from Ceauşescu's writings so that his own would be published. There was one simple criterion for publication by every author: the more Ceauşescu quotations used, the better the chance of being published. As everyone understood these rules there was no need for official censorship in Romania. The same sycophancy applied on Romanian television with the president and his lady on screen for more than two hours each day. Every hesitation or mispronunciation was carefully erased before transmission, but this paled in comparison with the technical difficulties of not showing how short Nicolae really was. French dignitaries such as the lofty General de Gaulle and President Giscard d'Estaing were a particular problem as they could never be shown standing next to their host. A similar problem afflicted North Korean television with the diminutive Kim Jong-il.

Unfortunately the Ceauşescus' admiration of the Kim Il-Sung personality cult had led Nicolae to model the Romanian economy on that of North Korea. Rigid state control stifled initiative and led to falling production – resulting in near-collapse of the economy. Food rationing was reimposed, and the country was brought close to a standstill by a chronic energy shortage. The people knew who to blame: the self-proclaimed 'Genius of the Carpathians'. The tyrants of Romania were now to pay the price for believing too sincerely in their own personality cult. Cut off from reality and blinkered by their self-created godlike status, they were unable to change their policies to match reality. As a result the Romanian people took revenge on the inept tyrants living a life of luxury while the country was on the brink of starvation. On Christmas Day 1989 Nicolae and Elena were caught while attempting to escape from Bucharest. They were summarily tried and executed. Their gruesome end was reminiscent of that of Benito Mussolini in April 1945 when he, too, was executed by firing squad. Where the Ceauşescus' personality cult had blinded them to the bitter economic grievances of the Romanian people, the cult of Mussolini was reduced to a farce when the Germans cut him down to size as a puppet tyrant of the Nazi regime.

A study of the career of Mussolini and how a personality cult can go fatally wrong and bring down a tyrant might well have helped the Ceauşescus to survive. After 1926, when Mussolini was at the height of his popularity, his appeal for the Italian people steadily declined. In that year the fascist propaganda machine issued a decree requiring that a newsreel featuring Il Duce in action be screened before every feature film shown in Italian cinemas. Unlike the later dreary coverage of the Ceauşescus' meetings with foreign visitors and speeches to sullen workers, Mussolini constantly appeared in dramatic situations all over Italy. Part of the appeal was that his speeches were exciting and full of optimism for the future of the Italian people. Delivered in a powerful voice, they showed his mastery of popular oratory. His sentences were deliberately short and his words simple and direct ,but although full of passion they were often bombastic. As he said himself after a rousing address to the people of Mantua in October 1925, 'Mine are not speeches in the traditional sense. They are elocutions, a contact between my soul and yours, my heart and your heart.'

Benito Mussolini never abandoned his pose as the triumphant saviour of his people, although the fiasco of the botched conquest of Abyssinia followed by the disaster of Italy's alliance with Hitler largely destroyed his credibility. The African adventure badly damaged the Italian economy, bringing hunger and deprivation. The personality cult of the great dictator crumbled with surprising speed as Italy was defeated and Mussolini overthrown by his own fascist government. Photographs of him after his rescue by German paratroops from Italian partisans bear an uncanny resemblance to those of Hitler decorating members of the Hitler Youth for bravery as the Russians closed in on his Berlin bunker. Shabbily dressed and with his coat collar turned up, Hitler appears an almost furtive figure as he limps along the line of boy soldiers, patting cheeks and gripping arms in an unconvincing manner. The fate of Mussolini was even more ignominious, shot with his mistress Clara Petacci then hung upside down in front of a Milan petrol station, to be spat at and kicked by a vengeful Italian mob. Hitler was aware of that and determined that his own Götterdämmerung would take place in the privacy of the Berlin command bunker.

Like Mussolini Hitler, too, established a highly successful personality cult that in the early years of his rule brought him both national and international appeal. Its success was helped by his arrival on the scene at a time when the mass media offered new opportunities for communication. The German press was sophisticated; nationwide radio and provincial cinemas were booming. Using the Mussolini experience as their guide, Nazi propagandists quickly established an even more effective personality cult for Hitler. To a desperate people, Hitler seemed no ordinary politician but a godlike figure from the German past who had come to save the nation and lead the people back to prosperity, self-respect and power. For this reason alone he was greeted with almost universal approval and admiration. As the historian Eberhard Jackel wrote, 'What they felt for him was an almost childlike devotion to a beloved father, a devotion that could easily dissolve into compassion.' As if to complement his incarnation as the father figure of a reborn Germany, his birthdays at once became one of the most important events in the Nazi calendar. A new national 'Fathers' Day' was created, which commenced with the modest celebrations of 1934, progressed to the interminable military parades of 1939 and ended with a final macabre celebration in the Berlin bunker as the city was falling to the Russians.

The myth of Hitler as untainted redeemer of his people was so successful that his mistakes were blamed, like Mussolini's, not on the man himself but on the time-servers within the Nazi Party. For this reason there was precious little opposition to his rule from 1933 until 1945. The German people remained faithful to the cult of Adolf Hitler even when it was obvious that the war was lost. People were therefore shocked and outraged by the von Stauffenberg bomb plot of 1944. When the Führer emerged from the Wolf's Lair he quickly went on German radio to announce his survival and condemn the conspirators. His appeal for loyalty was a complete success, and he regained control of the nation and the renewed love of the people. For the Germans to have felt nothing but sympathy for a man who had wasted the lives of millions of young men and had brought the country to the very edge of disaster was an extraordinary achievement and possibly justifies the claim that Hitler's was the most successful personality cult in history. The obvious similarities between the personality cults of Hitler and Stalin has been well documented. One of their biographers, Richard Overy, has suggested that both men needed and utilized ritual adoration and to be constantly in the public eye – if not in person then in image. Above all they presented themselves as messianic figures sacrificing themselves for the sake of their people and therefore free from all normal moral constraints.

No matter how successful the image of Joseph Stalin was in the Soviet Union, just three years after his death in 1953 Nikita Khrushchev broke the spell by beginning an address to the Supreme Soviet with the words, 'Comrades, the cult of the individual acquired such monstrous size chiefly because Stalin himself, using all conceivable methods, supported the glorification of his own person.' The speech showed how much had changed in the three years since the unprecedented display of mourning that swept the Soviet Union on the news that Stalin was dead. The nation mourned, and weeping crowds filled Red Square to filter into the Kremlin and view his embalmed body.

Strangely some of his victims appeared genuinely to mourn his passing. Some were grateful to the enigmatic leader who had guided them to victory in the Great Patriotic War; a minority even wondered how they would face an uncertain future without their charismatic leader, 'What shall we do now that Comrade Stalin is dead? What shall we do?' one young Russian lamented.

Ironically for a man who had been the centre of such attention Stalin was unhappy in public and chose to remain in the shadows. In meetings he avoided taking the chair and made little contribution to the discussions. When he did speak in public it was in the slow and measured tones that he had learned earlier in secret lessons at the Moscow State Theatre in the early 1930s. There he had also learned to use his pipe as a stage prop to enhance his fatherly image and to smile frequently. The theatre coaches taught him the value of inserting meaningful pauses into his long speeches and of gazing deeply at his audience at frequent intervals. Later Stalin introduced added some personal touches of his own, such as returning the audience's applause when he had finished a speech. Stalin gradually became a near-mythical figure, the myth encouraged by the constant appearance of his visual image, as seen on posters and display material of the time. Throughout the 1920s and 1930s as his grip on the Soviet Union tightened, his face grew in size on posters. When he first took over from Lenin in 1924, his face was always shown smaller than that of the dead leader's. Often he was depicted as standing behind Lenin, in every sense, but as his power grew so did the pictures of his face until they were given equal visual weight. By the late 1930s Lenin had disappeared altogether and Stalin was the single dominant figure in all government display material. The turning point was the May Day Parade of 1932 when for the first time the colossal statues of Lenin and Stalin were of equal size. When a film biography of the departed leader, *Lenin in October*, appeared in 1937 Stalin dominated in almost every scene as the wise adviser guiding Lenin's every move. In Communist Party literature Stalin steadily replaced Lenin as the fount of communist wisdom. In 1934 every schoolchild in the Soviet Union was given a copy of the great leader's philosophy, much as Chinese children would one day be given a copy of *The Thoughts of Chairman Mao*. This document heaped fawning praise on the great leader, describing him as 'the inspired guide of the proletariat' and 'the wisest man of our times'.

As with most tyrants the image of the leader was closely guarded, and all artistic representations of Stalin, or anything written about him, were governed by an official rulebook – *What to Write About the Life and Activities of Comrade Stalin* – that artists or writers ignored at their peril. In essence the myth of the portrait became the reality, shackling Stalin to his own contrived image and making it impossible for him ever to abandon either his pipe or his trademark moustache. Nor was his cult confined to visual imagery; by the 1940s the very name of the leader had been imposed like a brand on towns and cities throughout the Soviet Union. Apart from Stalingrad, there were Stalinsk, Stalinogorsk, Stalinbad and dozens more. One brave Communist Party member even summoned up the courage to write to the head of Soviet cultural affairs, complaining that the Stalin name cult had gone too far, 'In the end, this sacred and beloved name – Stalin – may make so much noise in people's heads that . . . it will have the opposite effect.'

Some commentators believe that the success of the Stalin cult was that it met the Russian peasants' traditional need to worship God through a single human being. Traditionally this had been enshrined in the person of the tsar, the little father of his people, a good and honest ruler who would protect them from dishonest officials and tyrannical landlords. Certainly Stalin looked the fatherly part, with his moustache, smiling face and gentle gestures. The image was further enhanced by his ubiquitous pipe, which proved to be little more than a stage prop to reassure the people, for he hardly ever lit it. The character presented to the

Russian people was that of kindly 'Uncle Joe', dedicating his life to providing a better future for his people. The national need for a constant and protecting presence, even in death, was astutely provided by the Central Committee of the Communist Party when Lenin died in 1923. His embalmed body was put on display in a mausoleum in Red Square, and soon became a site of pilgrimage for the communist faithful from all over Russia. In 1953 Stalin joined him, but, eight years after the Khrushchev denunciation had finally sunk in, his corpse was quietly removed from the Kremlin and reinterred in an obscure burial plot. Khrushchev justified the banishment by saying, 'The further retention in the mausoleum of the sarcophagus of J.V. Stalin must be recognized as inappropriate given the serious violations by Stalin of Lenin's precepts; the abuse of power, the mass repressions of honourable Soviet people during the period of the personality cult make it impossible to leave the bier with his body in the mausoleum of V.I. Lenin.'

5
TYRANNY DRIVEN BY PARANOIA

Paranoia has been the most recognizable eccentricity of tyrants throughout the ages. The tyrant's hypersensitivity to perceived insults or criticism has been universal. The cruelty provoked by this fear of being overthrown or assassinated was notorious in the reigns of such tyrants as Vlad the Impaler and Ivan the Terrible. Stalin was the supreme example of ruling paranoia in the twentieth century. The sheer number of his victims and the dominating force of his paranoia has led some neuroscientists to suggest that it had a physical cause. Among these is the American James Fallon. He suggests this paranoia results from abnormalities in the lower frontal lobe and the amygdala of the brain – the area that regulates fear, rage and sexual desire. Fallon wrote that in some individuals the amygdala can be so poorly developed that it creates an extreme pattern of dependency and that while a normal person can get satisfaction from reading a good book or watching the sunset this does nothing for someone with an underdeveloped amygdala. For such people this means a greater tendency toward drug and alcohol addiction and severe painful withdrawal that gets progressively worse over time, leading to malignant dependent behaviour. In this way 'sadists . . . become addicted to torture and killing; dictators get high on power, an insatiable drive that gets progressively worse or malignant with time'. Fallon adds that a tyrant, in addition to theoretically having a hefty percentage of the twelve to fifteen particularly aggressive gene variants and a dysfunctional frontal lobe and amygdala, has usually also been seriously abused in childhood and/or lost important caretakers such as biological parents.

For decades psychologists have also sought to explain the workings of the tyrant's mind, and in 1943 at the height of the Second World War the Office of Strategic Services, the precursor of the Central Intelligence Agency, commissioned a secret psychological analysis of Adolf Hitler. It set out to examine how his paranoia had evolved and whether or not his future actions could be predicted. It began by suggesting that his close relationship as a child with his mother had been provoked by his brutal father. It suggested that all the emotions he had once felt for his mother unconsciously became transferred to Germany. This transfer was relatively easy because the German nation, like his mother, was the custodian of his future – and that held great promise, if only the circumstances were right. Furthermore as an Austrian he felt shut off from Germany as he now felt shut off from his mother, even though he secretly wished to be with her. Germany became a symbol of his ideal mother, and his sentiments are clearly expressed in his writings and speeches.

Hitler's well-known vegetarianism also seemed relevant to his mental state. He agreed with Wagner that much of the decay of civilization could be attributed to eating meat. The decadence that resulted had its origin in the abdomen and resulted in chronic constipation, poisoning of the digestive juices and drinking to excess. Curiously Hitler only became a real vegetarian after the death of his niece, Geli, with whom he is said to have had a strange, even perverted, sexual relationship. In clinical practice, the report suggests, one almost invariably finds compulsive vegetarianism setting in after the death of a loved object. His later behaviour towards women is also closely examined. When Hitler was smitten by a girl, he tended to grovel at her feet. He insisted on telling the girl that he was unworthy to kiss her hand or to sit near her and that he hoped she would be kind to him. The report concluded that Hitler 'was involved in a constant struggle against complete degradation whenever any affectionate components enter into the picture. His behaviour was masochistic, and he derived sexual pleasure from punishment inflicted on his own body.'

More importantly Hitler's outstanding defence mechanism was 'projection', a technique by which the ego of an individual defends itself against unpleasant impulses, tendencies or characteristics by denying their existence in himself while he attributes them to others. From a psychological point of view it is not too far-fetched to suppose that as the perversion developed and became more disgusting to Hitler himself he recoiled and projected it instead upon the Jews. By this process the Jew became a symbol of everything that Hitler hated in himself. Increasingly he became convinced that the Jew was a great parasite that sucked the lifeblood of the nation.

Long after the Second World War Dr Fritz Redlich, a neurologist and psychiatrist, provided an alternative assessment of Hitler's general psychiatric state. He suggested that although Hitler exhibited enough psychiatric symptoms to fill a psychiatry textbook, including extreme paranoia, he most likely was not truly mentally ill. Hitler's paranoid delusions, Dr Redlich claimed, should be viewed as a symptom of mental disorder; but most of Hitler's personality functioned more than adequately. He thought that Hitler knew exactly what he was doing and went about it with enthusiasm. However, Dr Redlich did note that Hitler suffered from a variety of physical and psychogenic ills and debated whether the German leader's physical abnormalities, his hypospadias and possible spina bifida occulta were signs that he had inherited syphilis from his father. Hitler's rage at this may have fuelled his anti-Semitism and his obsession with syphilis as a 'Jewish disease', a theme he dwelled upon for ten pages in *Mein Kampf*. In spite of this there was nothing severe enough to explain his behaviour, and Redlich concludes that Hitler's crimes and errors were not caused by illness. Nevertheless Redlich points out his phobia of disease, his explosive rages, his delusions and his conviction that he would die at an early age. The psychiatric symptoms, too – paranoia, narcissism, anxiety, depression and hypochondria – are also clearly well documented.

A more comprehensive form of madness, no less destructive than the paranoia already described, appears to have afflicted the Emperor Caligula in Ancient Rome. The question of whether or not he was clinically insane remains unanswered. Some of his contemporaries, such as Philo, thought him no more than a vicious prankster. Modern psychology would probably diagnose Caligula as delusional and possibly as suffering from antisocial personality disorder as a result of his traumatic upbringing. Certainly his behaviour was bizarre – as was his habit of watching executions over dinner. As his reign progressed he became ever more confused; Suetonius claimed that he often sent for men he had already secretly killed, as though they were still alive.

His medical history is unusually well documented for the times and reveals that as a child he suffered constant poor health. His conditions included epileptic fits; these so concerned his predecessor, Emperor Augustus, that he appointed two doctors to attend the child whenever he travelled. Even as a young adult Caligula continued to have fainting fits and had difficulty keeping his balance, although this did not prevent him racing chariots and horses in the arena. The most significant sign of disturbance was in his speech: whenever he had to address a public audience he spoke in an excited torrent of words, shifting from one foot to the other, unable to keep still. When taking part in dramatic performances his excitement was again apparent. He often became obsessed with the part he was playing, adding impromptu words and phrases to his speeches. Being so highly strung, he had great difficulty sleeping; according to Suetonius, who knew him better than most, he often managed little more than three hours a night before being awakened by nightmares. Suetonius blamed Caligula's condition on a single event – a powerful aphrodisiac administered to him by his wife, Caesonia – and recalled that he would often hold conversations with the statue of Jupiter on the Capitoline Hill or would shout out challenges to the gods while brandishing a spear. Other contemporaries such as Seneca and Philo also cast doubt on the emperor's sanity and used words such as dementia to describe his condition. Philo became convinced that the emperor was insane – having endured a crazed verbal onslaught while being required to follow him from room to room. Modern historians and psychologists have speculated that Caligula was a schizophrenic or psychopath, although his apparently sane if malicious sense of humour makes such analysis difficult. His cruel wit never left him: for example, when a supposedly rich man was executed on Caligula's orders only for the emperor to discover that the unfortunate victim was penniless, Caligula exclaimed ironically, 'What a pity. He seems to have died in vain.'

Although Caligula was born into an illustrious Roman family his traumatic early life must have deeply affected his mental stability. His father, Germanicus, was one of the most able and popular generals that Rome ever produced who, before his early death, was seen as the natural successor to the reigning Emperor Augustus. Caligula became the darling of the army, and when the tyrannical Emperor Tiberius died he was elected unanimously to the throne. Caligula may well have attempted to take his revenge on Tiberius for the humiliation he had received at his hands. In one account of the death of the 77-year-old emperor in AD 37, Caligula, thinking Tiberius to be dead, drew the imperial signet ring off his finger and was greeted as the new emperor by the crowd. Then it was announced that Tiberius had recovered and was asking for food. Caligula was terrified of Tiberius' revenge, and ordered Naevius Cordus Sertorius Macro, commander of the Praetorian Guard, to go into the emperor's bedroom and smother him with a cushion. The commander refused, and Tiberius died naturally some time after

At the start of his reign Caligula was so popular that when he fell ill a large crowd decided to sleep outside his palace to follow the hourly bulletins on his health. The historian Suetonius claimed that since childhood Caligula had been an epileptic. The Romans called this the 'parliamentary disease' and were wary of it because it was regarded as a bad omen for any politician to suffer a fit while involved in public affairs. This had been true of Caligula's fellow sufferer, Julius Caesar. The Jewish philosopher Philo of Alexandria claimed that the illness was a mental breakdown caused by the stress of being emperor and by Caligula's new, hectic lifestyle, which had weakened his constitution. This sexual licence may have given him some form of venereal disease that affected his brain, but a modern diagnosis by the medical historian A.T. Sandison is probably more accurate: he suggests that Caligula was suffering from epidemic encephalitis, known to produce symptoms of mental derangement as well as paralysis of the eye muscles. This may explain Suetonius' claim that the emperor was constantly looking in a mirror and pulling faces. In contrast a modern doctor, R.S. Katz, has proposed that Caligula had developed an overactive thyroid gland.

The nature of the emperor's sickness certainly altered his whole character. Those around him noticed a marked change in his behaviour. Suetonius catalogued the new eccentricities, noting that Caligula had developed a moon fetish, chronic insomnia and emotional fits – as well as displaying the most appalling table manners. Even more disturbing was the deep paranoia that caused him to behave with unprovoked aggression towards those he suspected. Two prominent and respected citizens, Gemellus and Silanus, were ordered to commit suicide because Caligula suspected them of plotting against him. When his sister Drusilla died the following year Caligula became hysterical with grief, refusing to cut both his hair and his beard. He ordered that Drusilla be made a goddess, so violating Rome's convoluted religious system and giving great offence to many. This was further compounded when he began spending vast sums of public money on senseless building projects. One was the construction of a personal bridge from his palace on the Palatine Hill to the

Capitoline Hill opposite, so that he could reach the statue of Jupiter there. Other crazed projects followed such as a new Temple of Augustus, the Theatre of Pompey and a vast extension to the imperial palace. Outside the city two massive new aqueducts, the Aqua Claudia and Anio Novus, were begun and praised by Pliny the Elder as the engineering marvels of the age. With increasing megalomania Caligula even had a large Egyptian obelisk shipped from Alexandria and erected in what is now the square facing St Peter's in Rome. These extravagant projects cost far more than the resources available, and to meet the difference the emperor ordered new taxes on taverns, artisans and, irrationally, on slaves. Further anger was caused by a tax on all food sold in the city as well as levies on lawyers and even on the daily wages of porters. Even the pimps and prostitutes of Rome were now taxed. These measures may well have been the last straw for the people of Rome who were already shocked and baffled by their emperor's eccentric behaviour.

The public suspicion that the emperor had lost his senses was confirmed when he announced his new proposal to dig a canal through the isthmus in Greece. This proved an impossible scheme and was soon abandoned. Then, in AD 39, rather than use ships to move his army he ordered a pontoon bridge five kilometres (three miles) long to be built across over the Gulf of Baiae, now part of the Bay of Naples, and then personally led his soldiers over in triumph. By now Caligula was behaving with increasing irrationality. Having decided to invade Britain he prepared a large army for embarkation, only suddenly and inexplicably to order them to collect shells from the beach instead. These were to be carried in triumph to Rome. To their astonishment the senators were then directed to add the shells to the treasures of the Capitol. He debated whether to erect a statue of himself in the Temple at Jerusalem and to order the Jews to worship it. In the context of this strange behaviour, the well-known rumour that he nominated his favourite horse, Incitatus, as a consul of Rome is totally believable. At the time there was no provision in Roman law for an emperor to be held responsible for his actions or removed from power. A despot such as Caligula could revel in cruelty or indulge in the wildest excesses without restraint. The only way to get rid of such a ruler was to kill him, which his Praetorians duly did in AD 41.

Not as overtly unbalanced as Caligula, Hitler and Stalin were not normal – although they were not, as far as can be judged, mentally unbalanced in any clinical sense. The biographer Richard Overy has described them as men 'driven in each case by a profound commitment to a single cause, for which, and for differing reasons, they saw themselves as the historical executor'. In the face of such a sense of destiny both men developed an exaggerated morbidity. Stalin had a profound fear of death and as he got older feared what his loss might mean for the revolution he thought to protect. Hitler, too, became consumed by a fear that he would not live long. Stalin was obsessed by the fear of being murdered and took elaborate precautions for his safety. Every curtain in his personal suite at the Kremlin had to be cropped to prevent anyone standing behind them unobserved. All his official cars were heavily armoured and without running boards to prevent assassins from jumping on and shooting him. As a further precaution he never announced in advance in which particular bedroom he would be sleeping on a particular day. There were even rumours that he would not eat until his food and drink had been sampled by an official food-taster. When out in public his militia and security men were ordered always to place themselves between him and the crowd on the pavements.

As he grew older, even when sick and dying, Stalin's paranoia remained unabated as he persistently claimed that assassins were all around him. This suspicion kept his nervous assistants in a constant state of suppressed terror and fearful that one of them would be accused. In June 1951 he pounced, abruptly ordering the arrest of Viktor Abakumov, the head of Soviet counter-intelligence, for allegedly plotting against him. Then in the autumn of the same year, without even consulting his aides, he dictated a central committee resolution warning of what he called a 'Mingrelian nationalist conspiracy'. The Mingrelians were a minority ethnic group in Georgia, whose most prominent member was none other than Lavrentiy Beria, the head of Soviet security. Another wave of Stalinist persecution followed with the usual arrests, dismissals from government posts and executions. In the upheaval that followed the whole of the Georgian communist elite suffered, including many of Beria's close associates and protégés. Many thought that Stalin's real target must be Beria himself, but at the last moment he hesitated to attack such an important member of his own security service. Stalin's paranoia continued to grow. The next group to come under suspicion was the Jews. He told a party meeting that in his opinion 'every Jew is a nationalist and an agent of American intelligence'. Then in a last throw of the paranoid dice on 13 January 1953 *Pravda* under his directions revealed to the Soviet people the existence of a so-called 'doctors' plot'. There was, *Pravda* claimed, a 'terrorist groups of doctors' who were conspiring to 'cut short the lives of active public figures in the Soviet Union by means of sabotaged medical treatment'. Of the accused nine doctors, six of them were Jews. The innocent men were arrested and accused of plotting to poison and kill the Soviet leadership. At Stalin's personal instruction they were tortured in order to obtain confessions. 'Beat, beat and again beat,' Stalin commanded the interrogators. The unfortunate physicians can be described as lucky only in comparison with Stalin's 18 million other victims. The dictator died days before their trial was to begin. A month later *Pravda* announced that the doctors were innocent and had been released from prison. It later became known that after their pro-forma trial and conviction, Stalin intended to organize pogroms around the country, after which prominent members of the Jewish community would publicly beg him to protect the Jews by sending them all to Siberia. Indeed, when Stalin died the supposedly spontaneous appeal by leading Jews had already been written and signed; the signatories had been coerced into signing.

Later commentators such as American psychiatrists Robert Robins and Jerrold Post questioned the depth of Stalin's paranoia in their study of political paranoia, suggesting that he may have been a person who was not gravely paranoid but who reaped political rewards from appearing to be. The true criterion was whether or not the paranoid behaviour was relevant or contradictory to the ruler's political interests while remaining consistent with his fantasies. Stalin had revealed the paranoid dimension of his personality when he created the Great Terror of 1934–9, a purge instituted after he had consolidated his rule and was no longer politically vulnerable. In that case he expressed his desire to purge his own psychological demons. Although Stalin was never personally involved in the act of murder – as Ivan the Terrible had been – he was nevertheless responsible for the death of millions of innocent Russians. These people were executed, worked to death in the gulags of the 1930s or simply died of starvation as a result of Stalin's disastrous economic policies. Without exception his victims died because of the Russian despot's paranoia – the result of his own early insecurity. Stalin was suspicious of everyone, particularly his closest advisers, and was constantly looking for an opportunity to strike first. Even when in a position of supreme power, with every potential rival either dead or in prison, he remained consumed by suspicion. In October 1943 his old colleague Sergei Kirov was killed by an assassin, provoking Stalin to insist that the Supreme Soviet immediately implement what became known as the 'Kirov law'. This became his means of destroying the thousands of Communist Party members he suspected might oppose or plot against him in the future. The first to go were the late Kirov's own supporters, those 100 or so delegates who had applauded him at the last party conference. All were denounced as enemies of the people, arrested and either executed or sent to the gulags.

With the Kirov law, Stalin had defined the power of the tyrant in the modern state; his example was soon followed by Adolf Hitler in Nazi Germany. Now both tyrannies had a law that violated the basic concept of justice, making it possible for suspected dissidents to be executed without trial if it was deemed necessary for the defence of the state. From now on anyone who even questioned the leader's authority in Soviet Russia or Nazi Germany knew that they risked conviction and summary execution. Stalin's behaviour at the Kremlin kept many of his surviving cronies in terror. Later Soviet officials would describe the daily nightmare of dinner with Stalin as the same macabre ceremony was re-enacted each evening. Stalin would preside at the head of the table, ordering his ministers and acolytes to swallow drink after drink while he bullied, cajoled, probed and flattered them. As dawn approached, his bemused and terrified guests sat awaiting their fate. Often nothing would happen, but occasionally the NKVD would suddenly burst in and lead one or two of them off to be shot. As Robins and Post suggested, Stalin's behaviour was typical of a paranoid personality: Stalin was unable to come to terms with his own 'badness', rage and hostility so he projected these qualities on to others. Post described such men as Stalin when he wrote, 'Violently angry and afraid of their own aggression, paranoids defend against their rage by viewing themselves as the victims of persecutors. In effect, the paranoid's impulse to persecute and tyrannize others is denied and projected on to phantom enemies who then become imaginary persecutors who must be hunted down and either subjugated or destroyed.'

Paranoid behaviour was not confined to the tyrants of Europe in the 1930s. It was seen in Africa after the Second World War when Idi Amin seized power in Uganda on 25 January 1971. Again driven by resentment of perceived early injustices he moved swiftly to take paranoia-fuelled revenge himself on a country that had rejected and reviled him as a child. Only the British Army had treated him with any kind of respect. They had shown him a way out of the degradation and virtual non-existence of his previous life.

He began by having every member of his predecessor's administration seized and shot. He then ordered the arrest of many of the country's professionals – as Pol Pot did in Cambodia. Their crime was to have received the education that Amin lacked and to have prospered while he remained a reject. Then, in an African repeat of Stalin's purge of the Red Army, he had most of the senior officers in the Ugandan army arrested and immediately shot. Amin's revenge continued to be remorseless: the catalogue of terror he inflicted on his victims in those first days of rule is as appalling as anything conducted by the Nazis or even Ivan the Terrible. The chief justice of the Ugandan high court, Benedicto Kiwanuka, was arrested, his limbs severed, his genitals cut off and stuffed into his mouth – and was finally burned to death. A similar fate awaited the vice-chancellor of Makere University, who had listened to his denouncement on Ugandan radio and had waited impassively to meet his fate. Many of Amin's victims were first taken to Amin's palace where they were tortured and degraded. Amin enjoyed the whole process as they pleaded for mercy. Again, as in Cambodia under Pol Pot, it was soon obvious that anyone well educated or in a senior position in Ugandan society was in the gravest danger. Those left had to deal with a damaged economy and lack of proper administration. Soon even the middle-ranking bureaucrats and police came under attack with the lucky ones being dismissed and others simply shot out of hand. Now the only real authority in Uganda was the army, commanded by its junior officers.

A year after his coup Amin, again driven by paranoid delusion, celebrated the event by having more than 500 prisoners murdered at Mutakula Prison in Kampala. As the killings continued it was said that more than 30,000 people had been murdered by the bloody regime. Most evenings Amin would appear on the state-controlled television channel to assure the people how well

Uganda was doing and state that any rumoured deaths were the result of foreign invaders or unavoidable accidents; in any case, he said, such events were being rigorously dealt with by the authorities – all suspicious deaths were being investigated by the Ugandan security forces. In these broadcasts Amin adopted a casual attitude, speaking in a series of friendly harangues delivered with good humour. This joviality masked the horrendous truth that was only revealed after the Tanzanian invasion and the overthrow of Amin's brutal regime. The Tanzanians found a bloodstained drainage gully under Amin's house where prisoners had lain before being shot, so that their blood would drain away without staining the floor. Even the routine of the gas chambers at Auschwitz was less brutal.

In eight years more than 300,000 Ugandans were killed. Amin led the way in the brutality. He enjoyed personally decapitating his enemies, and on one occasion he and a few family friends passed a pleasant farewell dinner with the severed heads of two opponents propped up at their places round the table. He had the second of his five wives murdered and dismembered and then ordered the pieces be retrieved from a burlap sack and stitched together so he could show her off to their children. The expatriate community he regarded principally as a source of hostages – as in the case of adventurer and writer Denis Hills, whom he arrested and sentenced to death. Hills was spared and repatriated after the intervention of Queen Elizabeth II. Then, after supposedly being advised to do so by God, Amin expelled all the Asians and destroyed his country's economy. Finally he decided to invade Tanzania, and that was the end.

Amin's sadistic behaviour seems shocking, but it was not a novelty in Uganda. In the previous century Uganda, then known as the Kingdom of Buganda, was ruled by the tyrannical King Mutesa. His kingdom was visited in 1859 by the English explorer John Hanning Speke who was astonished at the brutality of the regime. He noted that any infringement of the elaborate laws was met by instant death at the hands of King Mutesa's body-guards. When Speke showed Mutesa how guns worked by shooting four cows, Mutesa gave a rifle to a page and asked him to test it by shooting a man in the outer court, which the page promptly did. From Speke's account, nobody around Mutesa even bothered to ask who had been killed. Court officials had to attend him at specified times on pain of death, and those who failed to salute him in the correct manner or whose costumes were incorrect were instantly executed. To show even a glimpse of bare ankle was taken as an insult and earned instant execution. Extreme caution was always necessary in the presence of the king, for to inadvertently touch his throne or his clothes, or even cast a glance in the direction of any of his wives, earned the same punishment. Every member of his court moved carefully in the presence of the paranoid monarch, for instant death awaited any messenger who walked instead of running to deliver a message. Foreign artefacts were banned for anyone other than members of the royal family. Anyone found in possession of beads or brass wire was immediately killed. Speke was fascinated by this horrendous behaviour as he witnessed these daily executions for trivial offences. One of the worst examples he saw was a young woman who had run away from her husband and taken shelter for a few days with a decrepit old man. Both were brought before Mutesa, who ordered that they be fed and kept alive as long as possible while they were systematically dismembered and fed to vultures. Later, as they walked together, Mutesa noticed a woman who had received the punishment of being tied to a tree. Taking the carbine from Speke, Mutesa shot her dead on the spot. Speke observed that this behaviour was not unusual in a country where it was the custom to burn alive the brothers whenever a new king came to the throne.

Violent rule was, then, common in Africa – as witnessed by another explorer, Henry Fynn, who visited the court of the Zulu king, Chaka, and saw that the king could decree instant death by the slightest gesture of one finger. Even on his first day at the court Fynn watched the execution of ten men, followed by sixty young boys – and this before the king had even breakfasted. The usual method of execution was to break the neck, but anyone accused of witchcraft suffered a more terrible fate being either hung upside down and slowly roasted to death or having a stake driven through the anus and left to die in the manner made infamous by Vlad the Impaler. These were daily events and included the massacre of hundreds of women for supposed witchcraft. No one was safe, for Chaka's mother, Nandi, had similar powers – as did every village chief. The most shocking aspect of this tyranny was the sheer arbitrariness of the process as death was dispensed on the tyrant's whim without anyone knowing who would be the next victim of his sudden and irrational anger. When Nandi died a large crowd gathered and was told to weep. Those who failed were beaten to death by the rest. Fynn estimated that several thousand died while Chaka and his court howled with grief. As a bizarre postscript any woman who became pregnant within a year of Nandi's death was summarily executed along with her husband. The history of such bloody events in other parts of Africa perhaps makes the despotism of Idi Amin seems a little more explicable.

Paranoid revenge on a society was demonstrated again in Libya by Muammar Gaddafi who forced a rigorous programme of religious conformity on his people – on what he considered a decadent society that had denied him opportunity and prosperity. In September 1969 Gaddafi and fellow army officers deposed the infirm King Idris and with US connivance seized power. From now on Libyan law would be based on the Koran and Libya's foreign policy would be actively anti-Israel. New laws were harsh: thieves' hands were cut off and women were stoned to death for adultery. All symbols of Western decadence such as alcohol were banned, and nightclubs were outlawed. The new leader became personally involved in closing down the clubs and theatres – as when he joined his troops at the Bowdlerina Club and walked on stage waving a pistol and firing several shots into the ceiling. As the audience rushed for the exits he shouted, 'This cesspit of Western depravity is now officially closed.' Libya was now an Islamic state. Gaddafi turned all churches and synagogues into mosques. A set of draconian laws was enacted in the name of upholding security, further undermining the colonel's claim to be a champion of freedom from oppression and dictatorship. Libyans suffered under his seemingly random dictates. He switched from the standard Muslim calendar to one marking the years since the Prophet Muhammad's death, only to decide later that the Prophet's birth year was a more auspicious place to start. Event organizers threw up their hands and reverted to the Western calendar. He also decided to rename the months. February was 'Lights'. August was 'Hannibal'. Given the conceit that popular committees ran the country, everyone was required to attend committee sessions called at random once or twice a year to discuss an agenda that had been suggested by Gaddafi himself.

In the late 1970s he eliminated even mild critics through public trials and executions. Kangaroo courts were staged on soccer fields or basketball courts, where the accused were interrogated, often urinating in fear as they begged for their lives. The events were televised to make sure that no Libyan missed the point. The bodies of one group of students hanged in downtown Tripoli's main square were left there to rot for a week and traffic was rerouted to force cars to pass by. To consolidate his power Colonel Gaddafi tried to eliminate or isolate all of the eleven other members of the original revolutionary command council. Strikes or unauthorized news reports resulted in prison sentences, and illegal political activity was punishable by death. Western books were burned and private enterprise was banned. Libyan intelligence agents engaged in all manner of skulduggery, reaching overseas to kidnap and assassinate opponents. Meanwhile he was cementing Libya's status as a rogue state by bankrolling terrorist and guerrilla organizations on an almost global scale. These included the radical Palestinian Abu Nidal Organization (also known as Fatah) and in Europe the violent Red Army Faction of West Germany. At least a dozen coups or coup attempts in Africa were traced to his backing. That set him on a collision course with the West.

6
THE SUSPICION OF FRIENDSHIP

What is striking about the many paintings of the Emperor Napoleon is his strange solitariness – even when he is pictured with others he seems completely alone. Mentally he is always brooding as if contemplating his unique destiny, often with his hand tucked characteristically into the front of his army coat. This solitary aloofness became more pronounced as the years passed and his power grew. 'Napoleon', as his old military academy colleague General Caulaincourt remembered, 'had acquaintances but never friends.' He recognized this himself: the emperor admitted that he loved no one, not even his brothers. For him friendship was an empty word. This lack of empathy could make him ruthless and lacking in compassion on the battlefield. During his Italian campaign he ordered some Italian officials executed without trial and whole towns burned to the ground and their inhabitants slaughtered. His own soldiers he regarded, as his secretary said, as 'base coins or as tools with which he gratified his whims and ambitions'. Later in his career when facing defeat, like Hitler, Napoleon was quite prepared to bring down the world with him. This monomania makes the undoubted loyalty and affection of his troops even after his final defeat all the more inexplicable, for Napoleon appeared able to trust his staff more than most tyrants have been able to do. Usually those who had helped a tyrant to power were destined to be seen as his greatest potential enemies and were required to make constant attempts to defuse his latent suspicion. Herodotus, writing in his histories around 450 BC, had given a telling description of the paranoid nature of the tyrant when he wrote, 'Pay him moderate respect and he is angry because your respect is not enough; give him profound homage and he is again offended because, as he says, you just fawn on him like a lapdog.' One has only to recall the dangers of those having to deal with Idi Amin or Ivan the Terrible to appreciate the accuracy of Herodotus' words. Judging the right degree of sycophancy when dealing with a despot has always been a difficult and dangerous business. In some instances it could become farcical; one notorious example is the occasion on which Stalin's audience continued applauding a speech at ludicrous length because each member was terrified of showing disloyalty by being the first to stop clapping.

Being close to a tyrant is a dangerous business. Even being a close relative does not save a man or woman from suspicion as Kim Jong-un of North Korea demonstrated when he had his uncle arrested, tortured and brutally murdered for supposed disloyalty. The barbarity of this killing was particularly shocking to the world, for it occurred not at the time of Ivan the Terrible in the sixteenth century but in the modern city of Pyongyang in 2013. Kim had clearly learned the lesson of history that a tyrant retains control over those close to him by remorseless terror. Prison and torture are not enough: only killing will suffice if disloyalty is suspected among closest advisers. Moreover in some cases the more arbitrary the victim the better, for in such a society anyone – even the executioner – becomes a potential victim. As Aristotle wrote, 'A tyrant cannot be overthrown until the people gain confidence in each other and lose the fear that a neighbour will report any criticism or discontent of the regime.'

The relationship of King Henry VIII of England with his minister Thomas Cromwell was so close that few predicted it would end so abruptly and violently. Cromwell was as faithful a servant as any monarch could ever have wished for, and he had the additional advantage of being a master of the black arts of spin and propaganda. He appeared to act without regard to his own conscience at a time when people still maintained strong religious beliefs. He ran an efficient spy network that was the nearest a

THE SUSPICION OF FRIENDSHIP

sixteenth-century regime could get to having a modern secret police. Anyone who appeared to oppose the king was seen off by Cromwell on trumped-up charges of treason or some lesser crime. In an age that was still largely Christian, whether Roman Catholic or Protestant, he unleashed a reign of unadulterated terror against the Roman Catholic Church in England. On Henry's behalf he masterminded the complete dissolution of the English monasteries, destroying art and architecture and seizing one-sixth of the nation's wealth and turning it over to his master, the king.

Yet this total dedication was not enough to save him. When he came under his master's paranoid suspicion Cromwell's fall from grace was swift and decisive. He was arrested while at work in June 1540 and executed the following month. Historians have ever since debated the reasons why Henry turned against his most faithful attendant. It may well be that Cromwell was simply the victim of a man who was becoming more and more unpredictable. What is certain is that Henry had been deeply angered by the farce of his marriage to Anne of Cleves; this had been arranged by Cromwell who wanted a closer alliance between England and the Protestant princes of Northern Germany. Henry certainly felt publicly humiliated by this marriage and became suspicious that Cromwell was plotting to bring in a full version of Protestantism to England despite knowing that the king was adamantly against it. By now the king was entranced by Catherine Howard and Cromwell's fate was effectively sealed; the king was persuaded by Catherine's Roman Catholic uncle, the duke of Norfolk, to get rid of Cromwell. Therefore the relationship between Henry and Cromwell was destroyed over an ageing monarch's infatuation with a nineteen-year-old woman that blinded him to common sense regarding his faithful servant. An act of attainder denied Cromwell the chance of defending himself and was executed at Tyburn on 28 July 1540.

Tyranny is a lonely business as Henry VIII had come to

realize. There is only room for one tyrant in any society or state and seldom has a tyrant voluntarily relinquished his position. Violent overthrow is often inevitable unless natural death intervenes and with supreme power comes the inevitable paranoia and suspicion of those around. The late Colonel Gaddafi of Libya was so paranoid and his security was so tight it would have been impossible to assassinate him. A plastic surgeon who had come to smooth out his wrinkly features recalled how he had had to operate on Gaddafi at 2 a.m. in one of the colonel's secret bunkers and using only a local anaesthetic, so great was the dictator's fear of being killed in his sleep. Yet every tyrant has always depended on a group of friends, relatives or supporters who help his rise to power and make sure that he maintains his grip on the masses. Members of such a group need either to share a commitment to their leader's beliefs, no matter how absurd or fanatical, or to be so bereft of moral sense that they are able to obey the most criminal orders without question. Their reward is the share of the spoils and an enjoyment of the often considerable power delegated by the leader. The problem for the tyrant himself is that men capable of doing his bidding efficiently are also the ones most likely to overthrow him and seize power themselves. Successful military commanders are particularly dangerous in this context, as Napoleon demonstrated when he seized power from the Jacobin clique that came to rule France after the Revolution. It was a lesson not wasted on Joseph Stalin, one of whose greatest worries at the end of the Second World War was the tremendous popularity of his most successful commander, General Zhukov, the hero of the Battle of Kursk. Lauded in the West Zhukov began openly dissenting from current Soviet policy – for which he was twice banished by Stalin after the war; all references to him were removed from books and his image obliterated from photographs and paintings.

Driven by a morbid jealousy Stalin carried, in the words of Leon Trotsky, 'an active, never sleeping envy of all who were more gifted, more powerful, than he was'. Or as another early Bolshevik leader put it, 'If anybody speaks better than Stalin, his doom is sealed . . . such a man is a constant reminder to him that he is not the first, the best. If anybody writes better so much the worse for him because *he*, Stalin, only he should be the first Russian writer.' Accompanying this dangerous jealousy was an insatiable need for flattery that was apparent even in the 1920s when a friend complained, 'I am doing everything he has asked me to do but it is still not enough for him. He wants me to admit that he is a genius.' Later Lavrentiy Beria, the head of Soviet security or NKVD, suggested that the only way he could gain Stalin's favour was by fawning on him like a dog. This was confirmed in exile by Stalin's daughter Svetlana who recalled that Beria 'flattered my father with a shamelessness that was nothing if not Oriental. He praised him and made up to him in a way that caused old friends to wince with embarrassment.'

Few tyrants have equalled Joseph Stalin in their morbid distrust of the entourage that surrounded them. In 1936, convinced that his power was under threat, he launched a purge against 'anti-Soviet elements' throughout Soviet society and the military. This 'Great Terror' was carried out by the NKVD led by Nikolai Yezhov. Anyone suspected of secretly opposing Stalin's rule was targeted. The victims included minority ethnic groups, religious leaders and members of other political parties as well as those who held government office at every level. The list of Stalin's victims among his close allies is astonishing. Not only did he order the death of his chief of staff and the political commissar of the Russian army but the deaths of the commanders of every military district. A further 99 per cent of all Soviet ambassadors and 98 out of 139 members of the Central Party Congress were eliminated. He completed this bloody purge by executing the two chiefs of the secret service who had implemented the deaths of all those just listed. Throughout the whole process he was completely unmoved. During the trials of his victims he often watched the proceedings from behind a curtain. Only the occasional puff of pipe smoke revealed his menacing presence.

Although Stalin presented an avuncular image as kindly 'Uncle Joe', this was a mere façade as he was always convinced that others were as duplicitous as himself. Anxious officials would be reassured of his favour one day only to be arrested and often executed the next. His own secret police, the infamous NKVD, later the KGB, had evolved from the CHEKA, the body that stamped out dissent in the early days of Soviet rule and imposed the edicts of the new government. It was a plan by the NKVD that helped carry out the assassination in August 1940 of Leon Trotsky, once Stalin's close friend and political colleague in Mexico City. Less spectacularly the NKVD carried out the day-to-day business of arresting and torturing suspects at the Lubianka prison in Moscow or transporting them to rot in the gulags of Siberia. These terrible places were as emblematic of Stalin's Russia as the Nazi death camps were of Hitler's Germany. The gulags proved an ideal focus for Stalin's corrosive paranoia, and he filled them with a constant stream of new victims. The total number of Stalin's victims dispatched in these camps exceeded those of the SS and the Gestapo combined. More than 2 million Russians perished under Stalin's direct or indirect orders.

A comparison of the Russian people's fate under Stalin and the oppression they had endured at the hands of the last tsar makes astonishing reading. In the last year of Tsar Nicholas II's reign in 1918 there were approximately 170,000 people in Russia's gaols and prison camps. In 1938 at the height of Stalin's despotic rule the figure had grown to 16 million – or one-tenth of the entire Russian population. On one day in 1938 at the height of the infamous show trials Stalin and his henchman Molotov together signed the death warrants of more than 3,000 prisoners held by the NKVD. Wherever Stalin saw apparent friends he also saw potential enemies, so that the terror reached from the bottom to the top of Soviet society; but those closest to the seat of power were in the greatest danger. One of the most shocking statistics of the time is that of the 2,000 delegates who attended the governing congress of the Soviet Union in the period 1936–8 only twenty-four were still alive at the start of the Second World War.

Like Ivan the Terrible Stalin was most dangerous to those closest to him. His early comrades – those who had fought with him to bring the communists to power and ensured his election as chairman of the party – were in the greatest danger. No one was safe. Stalin would use the most trivial accusations to justify the elimination of the most senior members of his government. To Stalin's twisted mind the more loyal a man appeared the more he came under suspicion. This perverse logic led him to murder many of his most able colleagues. Leon Trotsky, Grigory Zinoviev, Lev Kamenev, Karl Radek and Christian Rakovsky all came under inevitable suspicion and were disposed of. Typical was the arrest in August 1936 of Zinoviev, Kamenev and fourteen other loyal comrades. They were charged with belonging to a secret terrorist organization and planning to kill Stalin himself. If this was not enough they were also said to have been conspiring with the German and Japanese imperialists to betray the Soviet Union. Theirs was the first 'show trial' of the period and set the pattern for what was to come. In the following years thousands of innocent citizens were arrested and tortured into confessing to false and unbelievable crimes.

After the politicians it was the turn of the Red Army to be thoroughly purged. Dubious documents found in June 1937 seemed to implicate the high command in a conspiracy against Stalin. On closer examination it was obvious that these were clearly Nazi forgeries intended to destabilize the Soviet Union. At the subsequent trial of the 'conspirators' the only evidence produced was a series forced confessions made under torture. Yet it was enough to achieve Stalin's aim, the disgrace and elimination of the leading military commanders he saw as potential rivals for his power. The purge then spread down through the ranks of the

Red Army and with more than 30,000 officers and men being executed, leaving the Soviet defence forces in chaos. Not only did the depleted army then suffer a humiliating defeat at the hands of tiny Finland in the Winter War of 1939 it was too weak to resist the German invasion two years later. Indeed it was the chaotic state of the Red Army that encouraged Hitler to launch Operation Barbarossa in the first place. That Russia eventually prevailed and Stalin became an international hero is one of the great ironies of modern history, given his paranoid near-destruction of both his army and his administration

After the war when he was at the height of his celebrity Stalin remained driven by irrational paranoid fear that would have serious economic consequences for the whole nation. One example was a group of local politicians who in 1949 suggested a Leningrad trade fair to boost the faltering economy. Stalin became suspicious of their motives and chose to see them as a personal threat to his power. Agents and lawyers were ordered to investigate their activities, and the following year the leading members of the trade fair committee were arrested. They were arraigned in a show trial, found guilty of embezzling state funds for 'non-approved business purposes' and summarily executed. Yet Stalin's manic paranoia was not satisfied, and more than 2,000 of Leningrad's ablest civil servants – among them scientists, writers and educators – were dismissed from their posts, with 200 of them being sent to the gulags where they all perished in the wastes of Siberia. To replace them in Leningrad Stalin ordered thousands of supposedly loyal bureaucrats to move there from Moscow.

Still Stalin's manic paranoia could not be satisfied, and he demanded new victims. Now it was to be Russia's Jewish community. At a time when the Cold War was at its height Stalin's convoluted mind concluded that because many Russian Jews had relatives in the USA some of them must surely be spying for the CIA. At the start of the bitter winter of 1952–3 he ordered the persecution of Soviet Jews to begin. The writer Samuel

Kassow recalled seeing Jewish children coming home from school bruised and beaten and Jewish adults assaulted on public buses. There was even a rumour that all Jews were to be deported to Birobidzhan, the Jewish autonomous region in the Far East. Jewish celebrities such as the violinist David Oistrakh and the ballerina Maya Plisetskaya were ordered to sign a statement of personal allegiance to Comrade Stalin. This was to be Stalin's last monstrous act of persecution, for a month later, on 28 February 1953, he failed to reappear after a typical drinking session the night before. His guards and cronies were so terrified of his paranoid reaction that for hours no one was brave enough to enter his bedroom. Eventually an aide plucked up enough courage to approach the bed but jumped back in alarm when one of Stalin's eyes opened briefly to deliver a last baleful stare.

The Russian tyrant was not alone in suspecting his close allies of treachery even though they had helped him to gain power. Tyrants have always needed such a reliable group to carry out the repression required to maintain themselves in power. Often this relationship has been formalized into an organization of ruthless men dedicated to keeping the leader safe from his potentially dangerous enemies. Usually such men have been recruited from the military elite and have in turn employed a whole network of spies and informers paid and rewarded for identifying anyone who voiced even mild criticism of the ruler or his policies. In some cases almost the entire population colludes in spying on each other – as happened in Nazi Germany, making the task of the professional spymasters all the easier. Such informers work eagerly, for as Niccolò Machiavelli pointed out during the Italian Renaissance the more successful a tyrant becomes the more the people are inclined to protect him by informing on his enemies. The reason is perhaps that people are keen to be associated with success and are prepared to suspend much of their moral sense and to obey the leader's criminal orders as long as he appears to remain in total control. The problem every despot faces is the paradox that those prepared to do his bidding efficiently are the very ones who are most likely to attempt overthrow him and seize power themselves.

Nowhere was this more relevant than in Communist China under Mao Tse-tung. The French psychiatrist Jacques Andrieu has examined the peculiarly neurotic personality of the 'Great Helmsman' and his deep hatred of intellectuals. Mao's growing paranoia became centred on the man closest to him, the once beloved vice-chairman and minister of defence, Lin Biao. Photos of the vice-chairman appeared with increasing regularity like those of the chairman himself as their linked cults of personality developed. Then suddenly Lin Biao completely vanished from the Chinese media and there was no longer any mention of Mao's 'closest comrade-in-arms' and 'best student'. No explanation was given as the public became increasingly uneasy and tried to fathom just what the mysterious silence meant. Those at the top were then informed that Lin Biao had fallen from Chairman Mao's favour. Then on 14 September 1971 Zhou Enlai announced to a top-secret Politburo meeting the suspension of numerous high-ranking unnamed military officials. Self-criticisms were demanded of these people. This was followed by the arrest of ninety-three officers and purge of more than 1,000 of those accused of having ties to Lin Biao. It was in October that the news trickled down to the lower levels of the party hierarchy, and a month later the public received the grim news. At the 1980 show trial of the 'Lin Biao and Gang of Four counter-revolutionary cliques' Lin Biao was accused of making a bid to become chairman of the state and to usurp power; when a 'peaceful transition' had failed he put into motion a plot for an armed counter-revolutionary coup d'état. The heir to Mao's precious Cultural Revolution now stood accused of orchestrating a plot to seize power for himself. The public was confused and awestruck by these events. What did this bode for the future? What did this say about the Cultural Revolution that Lin Biao had come to symbolize personally? Mao's physician Dr Li Zhisui stated that Mao was so deeply shaken by the events that he went into a dramatic physical decline. He took to his bed in a deep depression, doing or saying little. When he did get up he appeared suddenly aged. Whether Lin died in a plane crash in Mongolia in 1971 while trying to flee to the Soviet Union or was killed for his role in the plot may never be known for certain, but almost the entire military high command was purged within a few weeks of Lin's death.

As well as needing individual supporters as confidantes the tyrant also requires a fanatical armed organization capable of carrying out the dirty work involved in securing the regime. These are invariably the misfits, the petty criminals, the psychopaths and the alienated that exist in any society and float to the surface during times of revolution or social upheaval. Such groups are bound together by mutual responsibility for the crimes they have committed. Early forms of secret police are known to have existed under the tyrannies of Ancient Greece, and similar bodies were later used by the Roman emperors and by the Muslim caliphs. In the Roman Empire, the duties of suppressing dissent and protecting the emperor became the responsibility of the elite Praetorian Guard. Originally the bodyguard of the Emperor Augustus Caesar this was founded soon after he came to power in 27 BC. Wearing civilian clothes enabled some of its members to blend inconspicuously with the crowd and to keep watch on potential troublemakers. Under the command of Lucius Aelius Sejanus the Praetorians set about eliminating the Emperor Tiberius' possible rivals and political opponents.

Their ruthlessness made the Praetorians the crucial power in Rome so that by AD 41 they were powerful enough to ensure that Claudius was elected emperor. From that moment every aspiring emperor had to retain the friendship and support of the Praetorian Guard by giving them a share of the imperial spoils and providing them with lucrative positions when they retired. Their power was again demonstrated in the civil war that followed the death of

Nero in AD 69 when the Guard actually chose his successor. As successive emperors proved to be weak rulers the Praetorians' influence continued to grow until they overreached themselves in AD 312. Their candidate for the imperial throne, Maxentius, was defeated at the Battle of Milvian Bridge. His conqueror – the new emperor, Constantine – immediately abolished the Praetorian Guard.

The lesson of the Praetorians for any future tyrant was that a ruler should be careful never to become wholly dependent on a single group of armed supporters and that the only way to ensure loyalty was by constant vigilance and the division of power. This would be the policy followed by Tsar Ivan the Terrible over a century later. He so distrusted the Russian aristocratic boyar class that he chose more than 6,000 foreigners to be his own version of a Praetorian Guard. These Oprichniki, dressed in all black and mounted on black horses, brought terror by night to the tsar's supposed enemies. A similar policy of trusting only foreign-born mercenaries was followed by other contemporary despots such as the Turkish sultan with his regiments of Janissaries. Composed of young male Christians captured in battle, they were trained as a royal bodyguard with exclusive and fanatical loyalty only to the sultan himself.

A man of violent mood swings, Tsar Ivan suddenly decided in 1572 to abolish the Oprichniki. Their mistake was to have become too powerful for their own good. Ivan had come to see them as a threat to his throne. These men were capable of becoming a second and even more treacherous Praetorian Guard and the real power brokers of Russia. Characteristically he acted with decisive brutality, seizing their newly acquired estates and executing such successful commanders as Prince Vorotynsky, who was accused of summoning witches to act against the tsar. Together with his wife, sons and entire household Vorotynsky was slow-roasted to death over a small fire – a fiendish method of execution devised by Ivan himself.

The legacy of the Oprichniki was to last long after their abolition. After the Second World War Stalin, who had read their history, made sure that all the new communist regimes that had come to power in Eastern Europe had their own secret police system based on his own Soviet system. Among the most infamous was the STASI of the East German Democratic Republic that kept files on an estimated 6 million of their own people. Such was their institutional paranoia that STASI members even spied on each other as well as employing a large section of the general public including church ministers, teachers and housewives to watch their neighbours and pass on unsolicited information or rumours about their neighbours and fellow workers – even their own relatives. The STASI model was followed among others by the Rumanian Securitate, which kept watch on the potential enemies of President Nicolae Ceaușescu of Romania. Again Ceaușescu's fear of his own people was such that almost 2 million Romanians were listed as possible suspects with 700,000 of their fellow citizens regularly informing on them. It has been estimated that at the height of Ceaușescu's regime as many as one in three Romanian citizens were either Securitate agents or acting as their informers. Yet in spite of this comprehensive repression spontaneous outbursts of discontent with Ceaușescu's cult of personality and economic mismanagement still occurred throughout his rule.

Repressive as these secret police organizations in Eastern Europe were they lacked the murderous fanaticism of Adolf Hitler's own Praetorian Guard – the infamous Schutzstaffel (SS) and Gestapo secret police. So enthused by their task were the members of SS that Hitler had no need to be suspicious of their loyalty or wary of them, as Stalin certainly had of the NKVD. The stormtroopers were happy to think of themselves as part of a divine mission to rid the country of the Jewish poison that had permeated German society. It seemed that the Führer could put his complete trust in these ruthless units, at least until the generals' bomb plot of

22 July 1944 revealed the first obvious signs of opposition to his rule. Meanwhile the *esprit de corps* of the SS remained impeccable as it carried out the most appalling atrocities throughout occupied Europe. The bespectacled Heinrich Himmler, looking more like a provincial bank manager than a mass murder, proved to be ideal leader of this, the most ruthless organization of any modern tyranny. Appropriately Himmler's dedication to Hitler appeared complete, and the Führer considered him one of the most if not the most loyal of all his close supporters.

However, even the faithful Himmler was to prove capable of betrayal when the war turned against Germany. Realizing that all would soon be lost he made clandestine advances to the Allies in late 1944. In complete violation of his principles this anti-Semite even attended a secret meeting with a representative of the World Jewish Congress at which Himmler agreed to the release of a number of female Jews from Ravensbrück concentration camp. This was in direct contravention of Nazi Germany's long-established policy. Himmler followed this with a series of secret meetings with Count Folke Bernadotte, the vice-president of the Swedish Red Cross. At these he treacherously discussed the possibility of a complete German surrender in the West. Finally in April 1945 the BBC broadcast the news to the world that Heinrich Himmler proposed unconditional German surrender to the Allies. When Hitler was told of Himmler's proposal he exploded with anger describing it as 'the most shameful betrayal in human history'. To Hitler Himmler's treachery was the worst betrayal of any that he had to endure. It was to prove the final straw. He immediately made preparations to take his own life, and two days later was dead.

Secret police such as Himmler's Gestapo have been a necessary part of every modern tyranny. They operate beyond and above the law in suppressing political dissent against the ruling authority. Unlike the traditional police authority who have the legal right to arrest and detain, a secret police has unsupervised control of the length of detention and can implement punishments independent of the law. Tactics of investigation and intimidation enable secret police officers to accrue so much power that they can operate with little or no restraint. Such an organization emerged a decade after the Second World War on the Caribbean island of Haiti, when François Duvalier was elected president. An intelligent man who had closely studied the careers and tactics of some the greatest tyrants of the twentieth century, Duvalier – known as 'Papa Doc' – set out to establish his own support group of secret police, the Tontons Macoutes. The name had a frightening resonance for the people of Haiti: derived from an old Creole word for bogeyman, it was traditionally used to scare disobedient children. Duvalier recruited his Macoutes from among the lowlifes and criminals of Haitian society. Each recruit was given a gun and some money before being set loose on his unfortunate fellow citizens. One of Duvalier's first brutal actions was to use the Tontons Macoutes to punish the unfortunate inhabitants of the poorest section of the capital city of Port-au-Prince, who had voted against him in the 1957 presidential election. One day a large hole was dug at a religious shrine near the city, and at nightfall trucks arrived full of opposition voters, gagged and bound hand and foot. They were thrown alive into the hole, which was then covered with tons of wet cement, smoothed over and left to dry with the victims buried underneath. The brutal message was not wasted on the other presidential candidates who immediately fled the country. Only one remained, the opposition leader Clement Jumelle, who was hunted through the streets of Port-au-Prince but who eventually managed to escape into the jungle.

The Macoutes had a low-key but distinctive appearance with their ragbag uniform based loosely on that of Mussolini's fascist police. One key feature was the sinister dark glasses that they all invariably wore as they went about terrorizing the country. With Duvalier's approval they were given free rein to rob, harass and even murder anyone in the country outside of the political elite, which they vigorously continued to do. Apart from acute paranoia Duvalier had something else in common with Joseph Stalin. As Stalin had utilized the religious beliefs of old Russia to establish his personality cult so Duvalier used the island's traditional mystic voodooism to create his. Images were widely distributed by the Macoutes showing President Duvalier dressed in a white top hat and tuxedo and wearing sunglasses. This was the costume of the voodoo god Baron Samedi who in Haitian culture traditionally stood at the crossroads on the pathway to death. Duvalier would deliberately terrify the uneducated peasantry by posing as Baron Samedi. Dressed in top hat and tails Papa Doc was the spitting image of the baron; the regime wasted little time printing posters that suggested that Papa Doc was as one with Jesus Christ and God himself. His endless harangues broadcast on the radio built his bizarre personality cult in a similar fashion. His most famous propaganda image showed a standing Jesus Christ resting his right hand on a seated Papa Doc's shoulder with the unambiguous caption, 'I have chosen him.'

As well as harnessing the religious superstition of Haiti to his cause Duvalier also exploited the country's inherent racism. Most of the Macoutes were black ex-slaves who bitterly resented the more prosperous, paler-skinned mulattos who controlled the commerce and formed the old elite of the country. Among the black population were the *bougans* or voodoo priests who were to prove particularly loyal to the Duvalier regime. These he encouraged to inform him of any dissent they might hear during their religious ceremonies. While most tyrannies have ignored women Duvalier was astute enough to realize how useful they could be. Thousands of poor black females were recruited to his armed female secret police known as the Fillettes Laleau. These ruthless female thugs proved so effective that some were soon commanding male Macoute units of their own. As supreme commander of the Tontons Macoutes Duvalier chose a particularly ruthless and vindictive ex-policeman Clément Barbot. A Caribbean version of Heinrich Himmler, Barbot gave the Macoutes an even greater licence to carry out extortion and murders in return for protecting the president. Some members even had private cells built in their own homes, literally turning law enforcement into a cottage industry.

The long-term problem for the Duvalier regime was that like Cuba Haiti was too close to the USA to be ignored. Under the presidency of John F. Kennedy the US administration decided that the crimes of the Duvalier regime had become so gross that they were prejudicing international opinion against the whole of Latin America. This might soon reflect badly on the USA, too, so a regime change was necessary. Moving swiftly the CIA sent agents to the US Embassy in Port-au-Prince who set out to identify any group of army officers who were prepared to stage a coup against the regime. Surprisingly the first to accept was Clément Barbot who many thought of as Duvalier's closest friend but who proved as disloyal as Heinrich Himmler had been to Adolf Hitler. Barbot began by using the American guns and explosives to attempt the assassination of Duvalier's son and heir Jean-Claude 'Baby Doc' and daughter Simone. When the plot failed Duvalier's revenge was immediate. Barbot was hunted down and murdered by his fellow Macoutes. When François Duvalier died in 1971 the regime passed to his son and heir 'Baby Doc' Duvalier until it finally fell in 1986 when the Haitian people turned on their oppressors, the Macoutes, burning their houses and attacking and killing them in the street.

7
THE NEED FOR A
RECLUSIVE NATION

F ear of assassination has always impelled tyrants to keep their distance from the common people, making tyranny a lonely business. The assassin's knife or fanatic's pistol awaited a ruler who allowed himself to come into too close contact with those outside his circle of trusted advisers. Extrovert public appearances by tyrants such as those beloved of the late Muammar Gaddafi have been rare and seclusion has often seemed the safer option. In some tyrannies the ruler has even attempted to sequester the entire country and cut it off from contact with the outside world to encourage it to develop in isolation. An essential part of this exclusivity was to ban foreign travel for the great majority of their people as well as to censor and closely monitor every form of communication between individuals. There was also a policy of forbidding intellectual contact and minimizing trade relations with other nations. Instead the tyrant encouraged a form of independent development by which the people survived and progressed without outside help.

One of the most notorious exponents of this policy of national reclusiveness was José Gaspar Rodríguez de Francia, ruler of Paraguay who between 1814 and 1840 managed virtually to cut his country off from all contact with the outside world. A keen student of the French Revolution, Francia was a devotee of Enlightenment philosophers, greatly admiring Voltaire and Jean-Jacques Rousseau as well as the French Encyclopaedists. Fatally like many later South American dictators he was also besotted with Emperor Napoleon and came to see him as his personal role model. Like many other tyrants of the past Francia suffered a disturbing childhood: he was brought up by an eccentric father in the company of insane brothers and sisters. Such early trauma clearly had a significant effect on the development of his personality.

The Paraguay in which Francia was born in 1757 was one of the least important of the Spanish colonies of South America. Small and poorly developed it had the additional problem of being completely landlocked between larger neighbours. Like other Spanish colonies on the continent Paraguay had become independent from Spain by the time Francia became president in 1814. Its main problem, however, was the proximity and influence of its neighbour, the far larger and more powerful country of Argentina. A man of great promise and ability, Francia began a career as a politician. From the start he showed outstanding diplomatic, financial and administrative skills. These gifts persuaded the Paraguayan electorate that he was the ideal man to run the country on independence. Once elected president Francia appeared to suffer a complete reversal of character as the self-proclaimed liberal revealed himself to be an authoritarian dictator who swiftly declared himself ruler of Paraguay for life. Once a reclusive intellectual with the largest personal library in the country he now became a ruthless man of action. With great determination he set out to transform his country from poverty into his own idiosyncratic version of a relatively moderate despotism.

So nation and ruler blended into one as Paraguay became Francia and Francia Paraguay. His need to control the whole system of government exceeded that of his great idol, Napoleon Bonaparte. Both the legislature and the executive became his sole prerogative with the inevitable consequence that the individual rights of the Paraguayan people disappeared as they were forced to obey the president's orders without question. His decrees were enforced by an army consisting of 5,000 regular troops and 20,000 militia. These men were given many privileges and enjoyed a lifestyle denied the ordinary people of Paraguay. Although human rights had been virtually abolished Francia's was an efficient administration. The national finances were carefully controlled and civil disputes continued to be dealt with objectively in the law courts. Nor was the corruption that often occurs in a tyranny allowed to develop in Paraguay. Strict honesty was required of every member of the Francia administration. As a curious precursor of what would happen over a century later in Pol Pot's Cambodia the monks were ordered out of their monasteries and sent to work in the fields.

Francia's determination to make Paraguay a reclusive state, cut off from the outside world, was most obvious in a near-embargo he placed on foreign trade. The nation's vessels that had traded along the rivers with neighbouring countries were forbidden to move and were left to rot at their moorings. Citizens were ordered not to engage in the import or export trades without a licence from the president and these were hard to obtain. The meagre imports that were permitted consisted mainly of guns and military supplies for the sole use of the army. A near-total ban on individuals leaving or entering the country was then enforced. In a landlocked country with a sparse population this was particularly harsh and an almost national sense of claustrophobia prevailed. All foreigners were barred and anyone who managed to cross the border into the country found themselves liable to be arrested and imprisoned. Among such unfortunates were three European explorers who were either ignorant of the ban or chose to ignore it. The three were colleagues of the great Prussian botanist Alexander von Humboldt on an expedition to South America. Entering the country by chance they were captured and thrown into a Paraguayan prison; it was several years before they were released.

Very occasionally and then only with the express personal permission of the president himself a Paraguayan might be allowed to leave his own country. To enforce this strange national imprisonment Francia ordered guards to be placed along the national borders to prevent anyone passing in or out. All contraband was to be seized, particularly books because these might contain subversive ideas. Escape was not easy; anyone who did manage to elude the guards then faced crossing the wild rivers and penetrating the hostile jungle of the area. Still for some the escape by river remained a temptation. One attempt was made by a French visitor trapped in Paraguay in 1823. He set off taking five black servants with him; they successfully evaded the border guards, but the attempt ended tragically when one of the men died of fatigue while another was fatally bitten by a poisonous snake. At this point the Frenchman gave up and surrendered himself and his remaining companions to the border guards.

Yet this strange isolation did have its merits, for it encouraged the development of a new Paraguayan infrastructure. Lost contact with the outside world and the need for self-sufficiency forced the country to begin developing its own industries. Particularly promising was the emergence of new businesses in the agricultural sector. Unfortunately a major setback occurred in 1820 when a plague of locusts devastated the harvest. Forbidden to import food from neighbouring countries Paraguay faced an inevitable famine until Francia swiftly intervened and ordered the nation's farmers quickly to plant a new crop. This second harvest was so successful that the system was adopted permanently, so doubling the nation's annual agricultural yield.

Under Francia's direction new crops were introduced: rice and cotton were now planted, not only diversifying Paraguay's agriculture but also starting a local textile industry. Although Francia's paternalistic rule had benefitted the national economy it continued to have a far darker side. The simplest principles of justice were ignored, and the country was plagued with insecurity as citizens were encouraged to spy and inform on each other. The usual signs of tyranny were apparent everywhere. People were arrested without charge and then disappeared before they could be put on trial. Brutal interrogation and torture were common and hundreds of political prisoners were thrown into camps or shackled in dungeons where they were denied medical treatment. Yet in spite of these violations the economy continued to grow so that by the time of Francia's death in 1844 Paraguay had developed into a strong and prosperous country – albeit an authoritarian police state. The nation was at peace with its neighbours and many new industries were flourishing. Most remarkably of all José Gaspar Rodríguez de Francia had remained popular with the people as a whole, particularly the non-Spanish and wholly Indian section.

The changes that Francia forced on the Paraguayan people were as fundamental to the architecture. The capital city, Asunción, had charming but ramshackle architecture with little uniformity of style and with streets that ran in a haphazard pattern. Francia shared the tyrant's common addiction to grandiose architectural developments and became obsessed with altering the look of the city with as much thoroughness as he already controlled the lives of its inhabitants. Ignoring the natural topography and without consulting any professional architects or surveyors he set out one day for the city centre with a small army of clerks and masons. Once there he set down a theodolite himself and took a straight line sighting to the horizon, then ordered everything in its path, including houses, trees and hills to be removed and a new twelve-metre-wide (forty-foot) street to be constructed in their place. On his command thousands of houses were demolished over the subsequent months, leaving their inhabitants in roofless misery. Anyone who protested was thrown into prison. Existing watercourses were filled in and the cityscape of Asuncion was ruthlessly levelled. When the annual rains came, large sections of the new works were washed away, creating chaos. The destruction was a classic example of the damage that the despotic power of a single megalomaniac can have on a people.

Asunción was not the only victim, for the attempt at national isolation came at a terrible cost to Francia himself. He appears to have suffered a remorseless mental deterioration, his behaviour becoming ever more eccentric. Like Ivan the Terrible he developed a crazed obsession with religion, which culminated in Francia appointing himself the head of the Roman Catholic Church in Paraguay. Again his obsessive compulsion to control led to him giving orders to ban all religious processions throughout the country. Paranoid fear then led him to insist that every Paraguayan church must be locked at night because the people might gather in them to plot his assassination. Finally a real conspiracy appeared when it was discovered that an old colleague, General Yegros, was plotting his overthrow. In a panic Francia ordered that every hedge, wall or potential hiding place for assassins close to his palace be immediately demolished. An old peasant woman daring to approach his palace to present a petition was seized by the guards and thrown into prison. Now even more frantic with fear Francia ordered his troops to open fire on any one seen staring at the palace. From now on he never left the palace unless accompanied by a large escort of cavalry. At the same time the bell-ringers at the cathedral facing his palace were ordered to toll their bells whenever the president went out to warn the people to stay inside their houses until the president had passed. Those unlucky enough to meet his cortège had to avert their eyes as the great man passed. Francia's own ending proved faithful to the policy of seclusion that he had enforced on his country throughout his rule. Before he died in 1840 he took to his bedroom and ordered no one to enter. As he lay dying, he became consumed with rage at his doctor who was waiting outside, and in a last fit of irrational paranoia he seized a sword and rushed out to kill him – only to fall dead himself in a fit of apoplexy.

A more fundamental and far more horrific attempt at creating a reclusive state was attempted over a century later on the other side of the world by the Khmer Rouge communists in Cambodia. When they seized power in April 1975 their leader Pol Pot set about creating one of the most isolationist regimes of modern times. In four years of Khmer Rouge rule an estimated 2 million people perished, mainly in the rural Killing Fields of Cambodia. Pol Pot's excuse for this savagery was that Cambodia was about to be attacked by foreign enemies and that both the USA and Vietnam were planning to invade and overthrow the hard-won victory of the Khmer Rouge. Pol Pot told the Cambodian people that there would be an immediate return to an isolated rural society. People were ordered to leave the towns; free-enterprise markets and even the existing currency were to be abolished. Every Buddhist monk was told to throw away his robes, abandon his monastery and go out into the country to live with the people. Foreign travel and contact with outsiders was naturally forbidden as Pol Pot set about executing members of the previous administration. The only commerce now permitted was through a series of cooperatives established throughout the country. Communal eating was ordered for everyone.

The worst sufferers were undoubtedly the educated elite of Cambodia for Pol Pot had taken Plato's advice to heart that a tyrant should keep a sharp eye open for men of courage, vision or intelligence and that by ridding his city of these potential troublemakers the tyrant preserves his power by allowing only the mediocre to remain. Tyrants have always hated intellectuals, realizing that they are the only group in society with sufficient intellectual and moral credibility to oppose them. So a murderous purge began with such professionals as doctors, teachers and engineers being arrested and shot in their thousands. Meanwhile the ordinary people were driven from their homes and villages out into the country. Living in poverty they eked out a miserable existence that was wholly dependent on the state. As the writer Elizabeth Becker declared, 'Cambodia became one great labour camp where workplace and home were fused together in a piece of land from which there was no exit.'

The new society was under the total control of local officials of the new regime, and people were moved arbitrarily about the countryside at the whim of a local commander. A great admirer of the policies of Mao Tse-tung Pol Pot then launched his own 'Great Leap Forward' – or a leap into even greater misery, as it became. The people were now ordered to labour in the fields for twenty hours a day and the list of the regime's scapegoats was expanded. Now every minority was under threat including the Chinese and Muslims and even the tiny number of those well-dressed, middle-class people still left. Khmer Rouge policy towards the outside world was almost totally isolationist. Foreigners were ordered to leave the country, and all foreign embassies closed. The national xenophobia led to a ban on all foreign economic or medical aid or assistance. Even speaking in a foreign language became a capital offence as newspapers and television stations were shut down, radios and bicycles confiscated and using the postal service or telephone was strictly prohibited.

Shops and businesses that had once flourished now stood closed, shuttered and empty. The Buddhist religion that had once sustained the people came under attack – and education was halted. Most destructive of all to the traditions of Cambodian society, the state now took over parental authority as Cambodia became almost totally sealed off from the outside world. Cambodia had come to rival the great tyrannies of the past. Prisoners were tortured and killed. As in many modern despotisms those about to be executed were forced to write their own 'confessions'. Poignantly tens of thousands of victims' photographs have been preserved – as have the piles of faceless skulls scattered throughout the Killing Fields. Such an appalling situation could not be allowed to continue and the Vietnamese army finally invaded the country in 1978, driving Pol Pot from power. When pictures of the destruction that had been wreaked on the Cambodian people reached the outside world, they were almost as shocking as those taken in the German death camps during the Second World War.

While Pol Pot was establishing his Asian version of hell on earth another tyrant was at the helm of an equally communist-inspired regime in Eastern Europe. Enver Hoxha kept his isolated mountainous country, Albania, rigidly cordoned off from the outside world for four decades. Hoxha derived his absolute powers at home from his positions as first secretary of the Albanian Workers' Party and commander-in-chief of the armed forces. He announced that he intended to lead the long-oppressed Albanian people towards a golden age of equality, true Marxism and most importantly complete liberation from all forms of outside dominance and imperial control. A nearly religious devotion to he anti-imperial tenets of Marxism–Leninism, combined with an unshakeable consciousness in the Albanian mind of being the slavish pawn of imperial powers for a half-millennium, caused Communist Albania to interpret the friendly adjurations of allies as just another external threat. A great admirer of Joseph Stalin Hoxha encouraged a form of national paranoia that left Albania with few friends abroad as his government broke with a succession of more powerful foreign benefactors and protectors. From the start he came with a clear message. 'Let everyone understand clearly, the walls of our fortress are of unshakeable granite rock,' he declared in one of the several books of memoirs he wrote.

In 1982 he further justified his determination to isolate Albania saying, 'Imperialists and their lackeys say that we have isolated ourselves from the "civilized" world. Both the bitter history of our country in the past and the reality of the "world" that they advertise have convinced us that it is by no means a "civilized world", but a world in which the bigger and stronger oppress and flay the smaller and the weaker, in which money and corruption make the law, and injustice, perfidy and backstabbing triumph.'

As one of the first communist countries to denounce the revisionism of Josip Tito of Yugoslavia, in 1946, Enver Hoxha visited Belgrade, hoping to appeal for more economic assistance and industrial planning. He was enraged to see the inordinate and unMarxist pomp, wealth, prestige and leisure of the Yugoslav socialists in their 'royal palaces'. He looked at them strutting about in their smart suits and glistening medals and decorating their offices with expensive Persian carpets. Poorly dressed Hoxha from poverty-stricken Albania was grossly humiliated. His backward nation's total dependency on Yugoslavia and Belgrade's 'parasitic' success using new economic prospects in Albania became apparent to Hoxha. He believed that the aim of the Yugoslavs was to prevent Albania from developing either its industry or its working class and to make it for ever dependent on Yugoslavia. Hoxha later cut his ties with the Soviet Union, too, when Nikita S. Khrushchev began denouncing Stalin in 1961. To Hoxha Khrushchev was merely trying to monopolize state authority by diminishing the cult of Stalin. 'Having seized state power in the Soviet Union,' Hoxha complained, 'the Khrushchevites set themselves as their main objective the destruction of the dictatorship of the proletariat, the restoration of capitalism and the transformation of the Soviet Union into an imperialist superpower.'

Having diplomatically isolated his country at the time of the Chinese-Soviet split Hoxha began to rely on China for material support and became a vocal, albeit increasingly irrelevant, supporter of Mao Tse-tung. Even this relationship began to fail when a thaw in Chinese–American relations began. In Hoxha's unflinching worldview Mao had been increasingly cultivating a revisionist version of Marxism–Leninism that opened Communist China to capitalist and imperialist decadence. Perhaps out of paranoia Hoxha interpreted China's beneficent philanthropy to economically unprofitable Albania as an ulterior means to an imperial end. Albanians were being imperially exploited or so he believed as a mere pawn and a staging ground for Chinese–Russian antagonism. Vietnam remained the only country with which Albania now had a positive, if hardly profitable, relationship.

Domestically Hoxha's objective had been to modernize what was generally regarded as one of the most backward countries in Europe. Although the Hoxha government was given credit for eliminating illiteracy it also repressed religion so that Hoxha could claim that Albania had become 'the world's first atheist state'. Unlike some East-Central European dictators who tended to be become less hard line with age, Hoxha had became more extreme and suspicious and intent on using his extensive security apparatus run by the dreaded secret police to penetrate the minds as well as the homes of Albanians. The citizens survived mainly by retreating into conformism and apathy, taking something of the paranoia of their all-seeing ruler into themselves. Predictably such a regime needed a scapegoat minority, and he found it in the Greek community whose members were ordered to change their Greek-sounding names to Albanian ones. Such a tyrannical rule could only be maintained by wholesale repression, and Hoxha presided over bloody purges and mass imprisonments of those opposing or not quick enough to obey official changes. Absolutely no criticism of or dissonance with the policies of Hoxha was tolerated. Routine purges occurred after each of Hoxha's self-defeating embargoes, seeking to liquidate supposed 'pro-Yugoslav' party members or others with Soviet sympathies. Koçi Xoxe, one of Albania's foremost politicians and one of Hoxha's closest compatriots, was executed in public for criticizing Hoxha's decision to split from the Yugoslav politico-economic orbit in 1949. Mehmet Shehu, Hoxha's closest associate and second-in-command since the 1944 war of anti-fascist liberation, committed 'suicide' in 1981 at a time when he was reported as being outspokenly critical of Hoxha's policy; there were unconfirmed reports that he had been killed on Hoxha's orders. Soon after the state newspaper *Zeri i Popullit* suddenly denounced Shehu as a 'secret agent of the Americans, Soviets and Yugoslavs' who had been liquidated 'because he met with the unbreakable unity of the party with the people'.

Besides concentrating on internal security the Hoxha government took steps in its last years to open commercial ties with its neighbours Greece and Yugoslavia although relations with them remained chilly. Hoxha was now keen to abandon his godlike status and to become a humble man of the people in stark contrast to the excesses of Soviet and Chinese leaders and even Kim Il-Sung in North Korea. Since the average Albanian had no ability to investigate the credibility of Hoxha's assertions or to compare Hoxha's cult of personality to these other dictators Albanians felt confident that their dictator was truly a gentle leader of compassion and empathy rather than self-aggrandizing corruption. Yet nothing was more bizarre than Hoxha's policy of building military bunkers throughout the country. These appeared in every corner of Albania, from mountain passes to city streets. They had little military value and were never used for their intended purpose during the years of communist rule. The cost of constructing them was a drain on Albania's resources, diverting these away from more pressing needs such as dealing with the country's housing shortage and poor roads. When communism fell in 1990, the hated bunkers were immediately abandoned.

8
AN OBSESSIVE BELIEF

Pol Pot had been driven by compulsion to eradicate the past and build a new unified Cambodian society. It was an obsession that he shared with tyrants of the past – not least the first Chinese emperor, Qin Shi Huang. Qin, who reigned 247–220 BC, was driven by the idea of a single unified Chinese nation free of foreign interference. At the time of his birth China was divided into six separate kingdoms, all constantly at war with one other. After a humiliating childhood as a hostage at the court of the King of Zhao he returned as a child king to his own state of Qin in 247 BC. Seizing full power at the age of twenty-one he began an aggressive campaign of unification, invading and annexing each of the neighbouring Chinese kingdoms in turn. His military successes were based on having superior military technology that allowed the peasant infantry to be the deciding factor in battle, so replacing the aristocratic mounted cavalry. By 215 BC Qin Shi Huang had achieved his ambition of uniting China and was the ruler of a nation so powerful that he was able to send an army of 300,000 troops to defeat the barbarian Huns who were threatening his borders.

In some ways the administration of Qin's new empire resembled that of the future Emperor Napoleon for he introduced a shared written system of justice – similar to the Code Napoleon – that was unique in Asia at the time. Other enlightened measures included the abolition of feudalism and the appointment of a civilian governor to control each of the thirty-six regions of the new unified China. Perhaps the most important reform of the Qin regime was the introduction of a single written script for the different Chinese spoken languages. From now on the spoken languages of Mandarin and Cantonese could share the same script, devised under Emperor Qin. At last written communications could be sent from the capital to any part of China. This made trade and administration far more efficient.

In such a vast country these reforms depended on a centralized and ruthless control. A national discipline was enforced to ensure the security of the emperor and his court. A new measure ordered that civilians were now forbidden to own weapons of their own and those already existing were to be handed in and melted down into ploughshares. In a development that anticipated Louis XIV of France in the seventeenth century Quin became obsessed with gathering all his nobles together in one place. Like Versailles Quin's new palace at Xianyang was used to keep an eye on potential troublemakers who might try and foment unrest. The difference was that residence at the French palace was optional while at Xianyang it was compulsory. Entire noble families of the defeated royal houses and their families and retainers were ordered to move there and an estimated 120,000 people were so relocated.

Yet Qin's obsession with creating a unified China came at a great cost to the national culture, and for this damage he was condemned by later historians. Ahead of his time he realized that the real threat to the authoritarian ruler was not so much the people as the freedom of ideas. Acting like an early Joseph Goebbels he ordered that every book in the country be collected and burned. The only exceptions he allowed were volumes that praised him personally and works of a practical nature such as medical textbooks. As a result most of the existing treasures of Chinese poetry and philosophy were arbitrarily destroyed. Particular care was taken to ensure that none of the works of Confucius escaped the flames. Ordinary people who attempted to hide or protect books were branded on the face and then sent to labour on building the Great Wall of China. Intellectuals who disobeyed suffered even greater punishment – for example, a group of 469 scholars was taken and buried alive. Those who discussed the lost books or quoted from them were summarily executed. To enforce these edicts Qin established an early form of the police state. Those who were aware of others' transgressions and who failed to report them were given the same punishment: the penalties for breaking the laws were draconian and included amputation of the left foot or branding on the face for stealing; treason was punished by the culprit being torn apart by chariots. Communal guilt was assumed in many cases, and if a single person was convicted of a crime he was executed along with his family, friends, old schoolmates and fellow villagers.

This barbaric assault on Chinese culture contrasted strongly with Qin's continued fascination with practical reforms, such as the unification of the currency into just two kinds of coinage, gold and copper. Measurements and axle length were made uniform, so that cartwheels anywhere in the country would fit the ruts in the roads; public works projects were initiated, including a system of canals for better irrigation and transport. New roads were constructed to link the towns and cities throughout China, making trade far easier. These innovative roads were indeed one of the great achievements of his reign, built to exact specifications – ninety metres (three hundred feet) wide and lined with pine trees planted at nine-metre (thirty-foot) intervals, they have survived in part to this day. There were three major highways, totalling more than 6,800 kilometres (4,200 miles) in length – even longer than the Roman roads that led from Scotland to Rome.

As Qin aged his preoccupation with a unified China was replaced by his second great obsession – the search for eternal life. Here he would far less successful in spite of the many and bizarre experiments on which he embarked. Finally he settled for a more practical form of immortality by commencing a series of epic building works. His first attempt was the Great Wall of China, which was followed by the construction of a vast imperial tomb. Before his death and believing he would rule for ever the First

Emperor decided to recreate his entire empire and court underground in clay, wood and bronze. Over a period of more than thirty years, around 700,000 labourers built him a palace for the afterlife. He surrounded this palace with representations of his officials, his buildings, his parks and animals – everything he would need to carry on his life without end. He planned that his body would be buried under a mound representing a miniature mountain, so that he would become an eternal part of China's landscape. It was completed just in time for Qin's death in 210 BC. His chosen companions for the afterlife were the members of a terracotta army composed of thousands of warriors. The last act of this obsessive tyrant was to order that the workmen who had built his tomb be entombed alive with him, so that its location would remain a secret until discovered by chance by local farmers in 1974. The terrible fate of these men was typical of the ruthlessness of Qin Shi Huang. This was noted in an epitaph for him composed by one of his own officials, Heou. 'Though he has suppressed the feudal lords and reunited the empire he is a man who received from heaven a violent, cruel and despotic nature ... only his judges and executioners can approach him and gain his favour while his seventy-five scholars of vast learning must content themselves with empty titles, for they are not employed in any work worthy of them.'

Much of Quin's violent and unpredictable behaviour has been blamed on his addiction to mercury. There was a belief in Ancient China that because mercury had many powers, among them the capacity to dissolve gold, it must have magical powers. To Qin these included the capability of prolonging life indefinitely. What the Chinese alchemists could not have known was the pathological effect of this liquid metal and the damage it does to the nervous system. Mercury poisoning causes uncontrollable tremors, but the greatest damage is done to the human brain. The victim suffers personality change becoming increasingly volatile, argumentative and aggressive. It also encourages the paranoia that was clearly manifest in both Ivan the Terrible and the Emperor Qin. Once in a bout of intense paranoia Qin ordered that anyone revealing his whereabouts should be instantly executed. After seven years of mercury addiction the Emperor Qin's kidneys began to fail. Knowing that time was running out, he began to plan his own funeral and accelerated the work on his magnificent tomb, which would now include an underground lake filled not with water but with liquid mercury.

While Qin was driven by the quest to unite and modernize his archaic society the Roman emperors of two centuries later had no such single and all-embracing ambition – being content to live in the reflected glory of past achievements. Consequently there was little need for reform within Rome itself that could be used by an aspiring emperor to justify a coup. There was also little need for overseas expansion for Rome had conquered all that it wanted of the known world. Not until the reign of the Emperor Constantine in the third century AD would a single ethical idea – the conversion of the Roman Empire to Christianity – be used as a justification for the seizure of power. Consequently the earlier Roman emperors had only their personalities or their promises of rewards to supporters to support any claim to the throne. There could be no appeal to nationalist sympathies for the only nationalists known to the Romans were barbarian tribes such as the Gauls and Goths. Inward-looking and selfish, these regimes were both politically and sexually incestuous, as power became concentrated in the hands of a few scheming patrician families. The rules of both Caligula and Nero are just extreme examples of this increasingly degenerate Rome; their fall was more the product of their own flawed characters than of administrative weakness.

Yet nationalism would eventually become a unifying belief used by tyrants for their own ends. None the less it was absent from the medieval as well as the ancient world. The Mongolian warlords Genghis Khan and Tamerlane ruled at a time when their peoples were driven by a common urge to conquer – not out of a sense of Mongol nationalism, but purely for plunder and out of the sheer exuberance of conquest. Nor were they concerned with building settlements but only with seizing transportable booty that they could eventually carry back to their homeland. It was not until the arrival of Vlad Tepes that territorial nationalism was invoked as justification for a ruthless regime. With the fall of Constantinople on 29 May 1453 the Turkish Sultan Mehmet II appeared to have the whole of Eastern Europe at his mercy, and he proceeded to mop up the remaining Byzantine possessions in the Morea unopposed. While the rest of Christendom wondered what to do about the Turkish threat, Vlad Tepes of Wallachia moved swiftly, securing his throne by uniting his people in a nationalistic and Christian-inspired struggle to throw off Turkish rule. The popular belief grew that the tyrant Vlad was the embodiment of evil, a fiend who tortured and killed on an inconceivable scale. He was, however, a pragmatic nationalist who led a national struggle against the Ottomans. Although he only ruled for six years he rejuvenated the economy and kept the country independent of the two neighbouring empires, Hungary and Ottoman Turkey. That version of Vlad came from the patriotic poems of nineteenth-century Romanian writers, who were fuelled by the nationalistic ideals of the 1848 European revolutions.

The most significant motivating idea of the nineteenth and twentieth centuries was a secular totalitarianism based on either left- or right-wing political ideology. The first modern invocation of this 'big idea' was the demand for social equality and justice that underpinned the French Revolution of 1789. It became the justification for the state tyranny that followed, its protagonists determined that it must be defended at all costs. As the armies of Austria and Prussia gathered on the borders to threaten the new French Republic, the Jacobins under Maximilien Robespierre induced the Convention to ratify despotic measures, thus weeding

AN OBSESSIVE BELIEF

out the supposed traitors in their midst. Their argument was that
this 'fifth column' would join the invading armies to overthrow
the hard-won freedoms that French citizens now enjoyed. As a
result of this national paranoia, more than a thousand aristocrats
and supporters of the old regime were dragged out of the Temple
prison in Paris and butchered in the streets, while the deputies in
the Convention began denouncing each other in the manner that
became familiar in Stalin's Russia of the late 1930s. A climate of
fear and insecurity descended on France; no one involved in
public life appeared safe. In return for the promise of a better and
well-ordered life, the individual was expected to sublimate his
personal interests and freedoms to total control by the state.

A far more transient idea than republicanism was the short-
lived nineteenth-century tyranny of aggressive expansionism
known as filibustering. Filibusters were independent adventurers
who launched freelance invasions of foreign countries, usually
aiming to annex them to the USA. The best known of these men
was William Walker, and although later generations would largely
forget him in the 1850s he fascinated the American public. Walker
was able to convince many Southerners of the desirability of
creating a slave-holding empire in tropical Latin America. To
many he was a swashbuckling champion of their 'manifest
destiny'. To others he was simply an international criminal. In
Walker's own mind he was a conqueror destined to create a
Central American empire. In 1853 he invaded Mexico with a
handful of men and barely escaped with his life, but two years later
he found his next target – Nicaragua. In its less than two decades
of full independence Nicaragua had suffered from repeated civil
wars, waged by the leaders of its two main cities, León and
Managua. The attraction of Nicaragua was that before the
construction of the Panama Canal it was home to one of the key
transit routes between California and the rest of the USA.

On 4 May 1855 Walker slipped out of San Francisco Bay in the
brig *Vesta*, along with fifty-seven followers. Although he spoke

little Spanish he demanded an independent command when he arrived in Nicaragua. He promptly launched a blundering attack and was lucky to survive. He then carried out perhaps the only inspired manoeuvre of his career. He commandeered a steamboat, landed his men in the rear of Granada and captured the city. Seeking to consolidate his power in the small country he created a unity provisional government with himself as commander of the army and Nicaragua's new strongman. Walker's arrogance alienated even his own puppet president, Patricio Rivas, who suddenly denounced him as a usurper and fled over the border. A northern alliance, consisting of Honduras, El Salvador and Guatemala, marched into Nicaragua, occupying León on July 12. Walker responded by staging a rigged election that made him president. He declared English to be the official language and issued an edict legalizing slavery. Then the Costa Ricans invaded again from the south. Walker knew he could survive only if he kept open the flow of reinforcements from the USA. He withdrew into Rivas, where the Central American alliance besieged him for months. Finally on 1 May 1857 he surrendered to an American naval officer, who conducted him and his men out of the country. Filibustering in Nicaragua was not quite finished, and on 25 November 1857 Walker landed again with 270 followers. In a controversial move the US Navy forced his prompt surrender. Walker launched a final invasion in 1860, but his luck had now ran out. The Royal Navy captured him before handing him over to the nearest authorities, the Hondurans, who promptly executed him by firing squad.

The later tyrannical regimes that followed were as conservative and anti-democratic as any in history. In practice totalitarian government meant the rule of a single individual under whom social or political change was impossible. These new leaders were much like the familiar tyrants of the past but rebranded by their supporters as men driven by ideas that could benefit the whole community. Their arrival was made possible only by the disillusion and despair that followed the end of the First World War. There was a perception, particularly in Central and Eastern European countries, that the government and the ruling classes had failed the people and that young men had been slaughtered in vain. These nations generally lacked a tradition of strong democratic government but retained a history of internal ethnic conflict made more acute by the steady growth in nationalism. When the new totalitarian dictators appeared in Russia, Italy and Germany they had the great advantage of being able to use the new sophisticated communication techniques of cinema and radio to promote themselves and their ideologies. The regimes of Fascist Italy, Nazi Germany and Soviet Russia used the forces of the state to repress discussion and dissent among the people. Put simply state terror would be visited on anyone who disparaged the ruling party or challenged its ideology. The result was a society in which the regime governed and controlled every aspect of an individual's life. Everything became subject to state control under the modern dictator – the economy, politics, religion, culture, philosophy, science, history, entertainment and even thought itself. This was the completion of a process that had begun during the First World War, when both the national economy and individual rights were subordinated to the task of winning, whatever the human cost.

The word totalitarian was first used to describe the all-embracing society of Fascist Italy under Benito Mussolini: every aspect of life, from industrial production to sport, was rigidly controlled by the state. As the dictator said in October 1925, 'All is for the state; nothing and no one are outside the state.' This was the most comprehensive definition of fascism ever given, and it appeared to many international observers that it could be equally well applied to Stalin's Communist Russia. What gave Musso-lini's regime its distinct character was its leader's cheerful commitment to violence as a state objective. Even before the disasters of the First World War Mussolini had in 1909 declared himself a disciple of the revolutionary syndicalist Georges Sorel and his theory of a permanent struggle between the proletariat and the bourgeoisie. Sorel believed that this conflict could re-energize society and produce a whole new system of moral values, but only if the state kept up a constant stream of rapid and profound social reforms imposed from above.

The biographer Richard Overy has compared the two greatest tyrants of the twentieth century – Hitler and Stalin. He asserts that while Stalin saw himself as a socialist committed to making the world a better place for workers, Hitler was perceived by his followers as a Christ-like figure who embodied in his own person the past and future of the German people as a superior race destined to rule subject peoples. As war leaders they greatly differed. Stalin's ruthless pre-war industrialization of the Soviet Union, at the cost of millions of peasant lives, made possible the avoidance of early defeat followed by the achievement of victory. Hitler, on the other hand, was a disastrous war leader who learned nothing. Intelligence remained the weakest link in the Nazi war machine, not least because Hitler would not believe its findings unless they conformed with his own instincts. The brilliant performance of the German Army was therefore undermined by Hitler's follies.

Having witnessed the collapse of Nazism and the disgrace of Joseph Stalin, Nicolae Ceauşescu of Romania was content to avoid fundamental totalitarianism. No great theoretical ideas under-pinned his inward-looking regime. He concentrated instead on promoting his own brand of pragmatic communism, combined with an unusually thorough personality cult. Yet he had one obsession that would earn him the hostility of almost all Romanians: what he grandly described as systematization. Sys-tematization was simply a plan to erase the past and physically build a new state. It required the total destruction of half of all Romania's historic villages, untouched since the Middle Ages. This proved to be state vandalism on a grand scale, and the national reluctance to back this grand idea of the tyrant can be seen in the fact that although plans were drawn up in 1972 the actual demolition did not begin until the late 1980s. Their replacement would be a series of new 'agro-industrial' mini-towns. These would be easier to police, and the freed land would be used to increase the woefully poor rate of agricultural production. At a time of international tension between East and West Ceauşescu's plan managed to unite both sides in opposition to it. Howls of protest swept into Bucharest from cultural and environmental organizations not only in Western Europe but from other communist countries and members of the Warsaw Pact. The underlying suspicion was that the real purpose of systemization and the destruction of thousands of historic buildings was Ceauşescu's determination to suppress the many ethnic minorities of Romania who lived in them. As these minorities had no voice outside the country and as their plight was being ignored by their own government, a Belgian organization, Operation Villages Romains, was set up with the aim of twinning every village in Romania with one in the West. It was hoped that this would offer them a voice and perhaps some form of protection.

The move proved to be remarkably successful; although there were gloomy reports of bulldozers flattening historic Saxon and Hungarian villages, only two were actually demolished. These also turned out not to be the homes of ethnic minorities but Romanian villages close to Bucharest. Their destruction showed what could have been – the inhabitants were given just twenty-four hours to vacate their houses before they were flattened and the land ploughed up; they were then rehoused in badly built apartment blocks near by. That Ceauşescu rapidly abandoned systematization showed that by the 1970s even a communist despot could no longer afford to ignore international opinion. Nevertheless a more low-key form of the scheme continued. In many small towns the old houses were demolished and the inhabitants relocated to grim new apartment blocks; and although the country towns and villages were largely saved the capital city of Bucharest came under assault from Ceauşescu's bulldozers. Still obsessed with his pet theory he ordered a quarter of the old city to be demolished to make way for a massive modern development. The entire Uranus district – comprising ten churches, some with exquisite wall paintings, three historic synagogues and a maze of old streets embellished by villas and small houses – was destroyed to make way for Ceauşescu's gargantuan new palace. That an area the size of Venice had disappeared, along with more than 2,000 square metres (22,000 square feet) of murals on the walls of the Monastery Vacaresti, did not concern him; it was portrayed as a benefit to the Romanian people. Like most of his despotic decisions it was taken unilaterally, for generally he was reluctant to delegate authority to subordinates and remained obsessively involved in matters of relatively minor significance.

This monstrosity of a palace was built in the already discredited Stalinist style. It was second in size only to the Pentagon in Washington, DC. The citizens watched in horror as it rose to dominate the Bucharest skyline. What made it even more distasteful was that it was constructed without regard to cost at a time when severe austerity measures had just been introduced. It was not in any way for the benefit of the Romanian people but solely for the personal use of Elena and Nicolae and furnished with the greatest opulence. Nearby was the Palace of the People, another example of monumental Stalinist architecture, standing on a new avenue lined with apartments reserved exclusively for the party faithful and the Securitate. This avenue, longer than the Champs-Élysées, was not completed before the Ceauşescus' fall; for years afterwards, the rusting cranes served as a memorial to the lost despot. Yet out of Ceauşescu's grandiose architectural schemes there appeared to come one final success. For more than a century there had been a dream of constructing a ship canal to connect the Danube with the Black Sea. Work had begun in 1949, but when criticized by Communist Party chief Gheorghe Gheorghiu-Dej five years later it was abandoned. The project had reputedly cost the lives of 60,000 convicts, peasants, priests and ex-landlords who were used as slave labour: housed in a Russian-style gulag at Capul Midia they endured a harsh climate, disease and beatings. Convinced that the project must be completed, however, Ceauşescu ordered work on the canal to be resumed in 1973. Employing modern machinery rather than convicts armed with shovels the canal made good progress, although it still required 30,000 workers and was the biggest investment project of its time. This proved to be a remarkable if temporary success when it was completed in 1984. However, three years later it was running at only one-tenth of its capacity and in the dictator's final years had been written off by the Romanian people as yet another of Ceauşescu's white elephants.

François 'Papa Doc' Duvalier of Haiti had a different obsession to that of Ceauşescu's systematization. Duvalier's big idea was that of negritude, a literary and ideological movement led by French-speaking black writers and intellectuals. The movement rejected European colonization and its role in the African diaspora and urged its followers to take pride in their 'blackness' and in traditional African values and culture. There was also mixed in an undercurrent of Marxist ideals. The movement's sympathizers included French philosopher Jean-Paul Sartre and Jacques Roumain, founder of the Haitian Communist Party. Negritude begun in the 1930s and had taken root in Haiti as a reaction against the materialism and crude racism demonstrated during the American occupation of the country in the 1920s. Between 1915 and 1934 the USA occupied Haiti and in the process killed more than 3,000 Haitians. Although the US occupation brought some prosperity to Haiti, it left the country with a 'doomed' financial structure. A $40 million loan imposed by the USA meant that much of the nation's wealth went to offshore creditors instead of being reinvested in the country's economy.

A decade later the young Duvalier joined the movement, believing that blacks like himself should concentrate on their blackness and their roots in Africa rather than model their society on that of the USA. As a young child Duvalier had to suffer the humiliation of his mother being declared insane and incarcerated in a mental asylum in Port-au-Prince. The stigma and shame felt by the young Duvalier implanted in him a deep resentment of mulattos, people of mixed black and white ancestry who formed the old elite of Haiti, the Roman Catholic Church and foreigners in general which he outlined in an ideological tract. The journal of negritude, *Les Griots*, championed this *noirisme* and called for the black people to assert their innate superiority over the mulattoes who had traditionally ruled Haiti. Part of this belief involved the rejection of the white man's Christianity and the promotion of African-derived voodooism as the true religion of the people. Duvalier's writings at this time give a clear indication of how he would implement negritude should he come to power – they are as firmly described as Hitler's resolve to destroy the Jews in *Mein Kampf*. Once elected president Duvalier moved swiftly to implement his policy by dismissing those of mixed race from positions of power and putting his black supporters in their place. Papa Doc was elected as president in 1957, although this is regarded by historians as a rigged election. The man who had ensconced himself in black pride and voodoo now had an entire country to run. The megalomania that had been carefully cultivated over the years was now ready to take centre stage.

Throughout his reign Papa Doc was known for routinely torturing any dissidents who opposed his rule. Perhaps much like modern North Korea's Kim Jong-un, Papa Doc Duvalier so antagonized what he considered his adversaries that he ended up isolating his country in a state of worse poverty than before. For many of the poorer blacks Papa Doc remained a hero with his message of black pride. Poor and subjugated already by these former oppressors many of his most ardent followers did not have much invested in the past structure of Haiti. A person who seemed to speak to their oppression was very welcome. So the supporters of Duvalier and negritude remained faithful despite the country falling into even greater destitution; Duvalier's machinations of corruption created a nascent, though fragile, black middle class. This limited success helped to maintain Duvalier's pose of being of an effective president. It was a legacy that he would pass on to his son, Jean-Claude 'Baby Doc' Duvalier, on his death in 1971.

9

BLIND ARROGANCE

On 2 December 1804 six thousand dignitaries and diplomats attending a ceremony inside Notre Dame Cathedral in Paris and witnessed the culmination of an extraordinary man's rise to total power from relatively humble origins. In an imperial extravaganza costing the nation millions of francs, Napoleon Bonaparte became Napoleon I 'by the grace of God and the Constitution of the Republic, Emperor of the French'. The ambitious military careerist, supporter of the French Revolution, hero of the 1796–7 Italian campaigns and First Consul now elevated himself above the hereditary monarchs whose *ancien régime* he had rigorously opposed a few years earlier. Just being a 'king' was simply not good enough for a man with such overweening ambition. He must emulate Charlemagne's example and be an emperor. Three months before his imperial coronation Napoleon visited Charlemagne's tomb at Aachen and spent time there in meditation. His fascination with the 'father of Europe' was profound almost to the point of imagined reincarnation. A few years later in 1809 he told some papal representatives, 'Take a good look at me. In me you see Charlemagne.'

At the high point of the ceremony Napoleon made a dramatic move: seizing the crown from the Pope's hands he placed it on his own head. It was one of the most arrogant gestures in history. Some of the French approved. The novelist Stendhal wrote, 'I am filled with a kind of religious sense merely by daring to write the first sentence in the history of Napoleon. He is quite simply the greatest man who has come into the world since Julius Caesar.' Yet even being an emperor was insufficient for Napoleon, and he complained that the French people were most unlikely ever to worship him as a god – as he really deserved. 'Look at Alexander,' he said, 'when he had conquered Asia and presented himself to the nations . . . the whole Orient believed him . . . but if I announced that, every fishwife would hoot when she saw me pass by. The masses are too enlightened these days; nothing great can be done any more.' Such was Napoleon's conviction that he should enjoy a godlike status that one of his courtiers thought he even believed that he could conquer the whole world. In this belief were the seeds of his downfall.

As well as arrogance Napoleon had an incredible amount of energy. He would hardly sleep at night and would take short naps throughout the day. Even so he worked almost twenty-four hours a day and was a poor delegator of responsibilities, preferring to micromanage everything himself. He believed that the only way to gain the esteem of the French people was to wage war continually and bring glory to his nation. This may have worked at first, but it turned sour in the end. This is no different from a leader using a strategy that worked in the past regardless of whether it is relevant in the present. After conquering a large portion of Europe, he installed most of his siblings on the throne of conquered lands. Rather than maintain the ideals of the French Revolution, which was the reason he was able to rise so high without noble credentials, he fell back on the idea of rewarding birth rather than skill. Worst of all when his closest advisers told him not to invade Russia in 1812 he chose not to listen. This cost him more than 500,000 men – and his downfall.

Like many tyrants Napoleon suffered from a manic ego that needed constant praise from those around him. His aides and advisers were therefore chosen as much for their eagerness to supply this as for their competence. A jealousy of anyone possessing an ability that rivalled his own had a crippling effect on his regime. One minister said that once emperor Napoleon conceived the idea of 'moulding a generation of satellites'. This involved establishing a pool of 500 young men under the age of forty who could be placed in administrative roles whenever vacancies occurred. Chosen for their enthusiasm for the emperor as much as for their innate talents, they often performed badly. These 'yes' men compromised his earlier military achievements, for, as another of his ministers said, 'all about him were timid and passive'. It was a mistake that would later be repeated by Hitler and Stalin. If Napoleon's arrogance compromised his domestic regime it also led to his downfall internationally. When in 1805 he thought Austria was arming against him he threatened to 'pay her a little visit with 200,000 men which she will not soon forget'. He then made it clear that he intended to dethrone Europe's old ruling houses and boasted to the Austrian Count Metternich that within ten years his would be the most ancient dynasty in Europe. The megalomania continued as when he conceived the idea of a Europe-wide trading block on English shipping without taking into account the ruinous effect on every nation involved. So the follies continued: the invasion of Spain, the imprisonment of the Pope that alienated Roman Catholics everywhere and militarily worst of all the invasion of Russia. Napoleon suffered the consequence of tyrannical arrogance because of his lack of critical self-judgement. He saw the society around him as nothing more than an extension of his own will; in many cases this leads to a blinding arrogance and an inability to judge events objectively, which results in a tyrant's downfall.

This was the fate suffered far earlier by the Roman emperors Nero and Caligula who also displayed a blind arrogance. It appears that both Caligula and Nero suffered from acute vanity owing to their overwhelming insecurities. To appease this insecurity both men asserted themselves superior to their pre-decessors rather than honouring them. Caligula and Nero violated the precedence of Augustus by disrespecting the Senate and pursuing a civil policy defined by cruelty and corruption. From the start of his reign Caligula, Gaius Julius Caesar Augustus Germanicus, behaved with disturbing perversity. Visiting a

Roman legion stationed on the Rhine that twenty-four years earlier had rebelled against his father, Germanicus, he arbitrarily decided to decimate it. This involved the regiment being drawn up on parade, lots drawn and an unlucky one in ten men being clubbed to death by their comrades. Before the sentence could be carried out, however, the angry soldiers began to rebel, and Caligula was forced to escape back to Rome. When news of this event spread it was the arbitrariness of Caligula's action rather than the brutality that shocked the Roman people.

Historians have for centuries debated whether or not Caligula was insane. Seneca, who knew Caligula personally and was thus writing contemporaneously about him, records absolutely nothing that would suggest he was mad; another contemporary author, Philo, did not hesitate to call Caligula a madman. Modern psychiatrists such as Elizabeth Ford have clinically diagnosed Caligula as a man suffering from bipolar personality disorder, which is characterized by prolonged periods of mania and depression. Although this diagnosis is possible it cannot explain his strange behaviour in chatting with the gods or bestowing honours on his horse. One explanation for the emperor's irrational arrogance may be his health: Suetonius does mention that Augustus was concerned enough about Caligula's health in AD 14 to provide him with two doctors for his epileptic seizures. The sources also claim that he had insomnia, suffered from horrible nightmares, hid under his bed during thunderstorms and had fainting spells and other ailments. He then suffered a more serious illness in AD 37. After experiencing a series of epileptic fits Caligula became convinced that he was about to die and willed the Roman Empire and his personal wealth over to his sister Drusilla. Much to his surprise he recovered and, believing that he had overcome death itself, began to consider himself invincible.

A near-death experience can lead to a person feeling that they have something important to accomplish in life. So it may have been with Caligula: convinced of his invulnerability he began to persecute some of the wealthiest families in the city seizing their property after randomly accusing them of treason. Members of the Senate attracted his particular attention. Those arrested were tortured before being painfully executed. Caligula revealed his innate sadism by forcing parents to witness their children's executions in his presence while he mocked their suffering. This sadism had its origins in his own dangerous and miserable childhood on the island of Capri where he suffered the tyranny and sexual perversions of his predecessor, Emperor Tiberius. This outrageous behaviour was part of what appeared to be his arrogant assault on the conventional respectability of Roman society. Caligula appeared determined to shock and to demonstrate his contempt for what passed as Roman morality. One gesture that outraged convention was the opening of a brothel within the walls of his own palace. The first customers ordered to attend were terrified senators and their spouses. Caligula took each wife in turn into his private bedroom before returning to recount to the humiliated husbands in great detail what sexual acts had taken place. This event alone sealed Caligula's eventual fate. The story of Caligula's outrageous action was recorded by the writer Suetonius who wrote that 'Such opposed vices, both the greatest arrogance and the greatest timidity, were to be found in the same person.' For all his arrogance Caligula could also display cowardice in some situations – such as his attempt to decimate the legion. Suetonius also agreed that much of Caligula's appalling behaviour had its roots in childhood insecurity and this led him to disrespect the Senate and to pursue a civil policy defined by cruelty and corruption.

Caligula was also arrogant in receiving titles. He saw himself as the Xerxes or Alexander the Great of his time. This unreal sense of self was compounded when began to 'claim for himself the majesty of a god'. Suetonius was disgusted that Caligula proclaimed his new divinity by removing the heads of the statues of Zeus and other gods and replacing them with his own. This disrespect towards the gods exposed his vanity and led Suetonius to comment reproachfully that 'this practice never conformed to the traditional manner of Roman citizens'. The delusion continued and in AD 40 Caligula began appearing in public dressed as various gods and demigods such as Hercules, Mercury, Venus and Apollo. His divine creation even extended to the empire, and he is said to have ordered that he be worshipped in Egypt as Neos Helios or the new sun god. Indeed he was represented as a sun god on Egyptian coins. Reportedly he began referring to himself as a god when meeting with politicians and he insisted that he be referred to as Jupiter on occasion in public documents. His new divine status had to be recognized throughout the Roman Empire and a sacred precinct was set apart for his worship at Miletus. Already in Rome itself two temples had been erected for his worship. One, that of Castor and Pollux on the Forum, was now linked directly to the Imperial residence on the Palatine and dedicated to Caligula. Here the emperor would occasionally appear and present himself to the people as the city god of Rome. By now Caligula's conceit dominated every aspect of his rule. On military campaign he ordered boats to be strung right across the Bay of Naples so that he could walk across them from one side to the other. Caligula's erratic behaviour, which also included ordering troops to gather seashells during a campaign against Britain, led many to question his sanity. Deliverance from his tyranny came in January AD 41 when members of the Praetorian Guard stabbed him to death in the corridor of his palace. Their leader was Cassius Chaerea, an officer Caligula had mocked for effeminacy before the whole court.

Arrogance such as Caligula's was often a feature of tyrannical rule, and it continued throughout the centuries – even after the overthrow of the European dictators in the twentieth century. Nor was it only the nominally Christian societies that produced tyrants. In India Akbar, the third generation Mughal emperor who lived from 1542 to 1605, proved to be the equal of any in his arrogance. He had neither love nor compassion for Hindus who were openly despised and contemptuously treated under his fanatical rule. Akbar was only one of the many despotic and cruel Mughal rulers in India, but he enforced the tradition of his forefathers with sincerity and equal ruthlessness. His life was full of acts of cruelty, barbarous actions and lust for women and wine. Considering the background in which Akbar was brought up and the environment in which he lived it was a surprise that he could ever have developed qualities of compassion. Yet his sycophantic courtiers, including the court chroniclers, gave him all the praise he desired – portraying him as a tolerant, secular and altruistic king. Later accounts of his life were closer to the truth showing his callousness and lack of concern for his subjects that led to untold misery in the form of famines and pestilence. Wars, revolts and rebellions constantly erupted throughout his reign, and there was no peace, let alone material and spiritual prosperity. He was also shown to be an avaricious miser who wasted vast sums on creating expensive buildings and mansions. Morality and humanitarian principles took a back seat to self-aggrandizement and lechery. After the capture of the city of Chittor Akbar, exasperated by the obstinate resistance it had offered, treated the town and garrison with merciless severity. The 8,000-strong Rajput garrison having been zealously helped during the siege by 40,000 peasants, the emperor ordered a general massacre that resulted in the death of 30,000. Akbar demanded the excision of one man's tongue, the trampling of opponents to death by elephants and other private or informal executions and assassinations.

That tyrants' blind arrogance was a universal phenomenon was shown by events in Central and South America, too, where a particularly unpleasant manifestation appeared in the Dominican Republic in 1930. Here an army officer, Rafael Trujillo, used troops to seize power in a coup d'état. Three weeks after he became president a powerful hurricane hit Santo Domingo leaving more than 3,000 dead. With relief money from the American Red

Cross he gained great credit by efficiently rebuilding the city. Trujillo had little interest in political theory but held a great admiration for Benito Mussolini and his flamboyant regime in Italy. When he came to power Trujillo had been a typical Dominican *caudillo* or warlord. He ran the country like a mafia fiefdom under the benevolent eye of the USA, which fully approved of his anti-communist stance. With US encouragement he banned the Dominican Communist Party soon after the start of the Cold War, and in return Washington was prepared to ignore the iniquities of his corrupt regime.

Without US interference Trujillo set about building himself a monstrous personality cult that contrasted markedly with both his physical stature and the strategic importance of his country. When he presented himself to the people at interminable military parades he always wore military uniform, decked out in gold braid and garish decorations. His overweening conceit required that the highest mountain in the country become Pico Trujillo; the capital city, Santo Domingo, was renamed Ciudad Trujillo and embellished with dozens of new civic buildings of doubtful architectural merit. The obligatory statues of Trujillo, an estimated 100,000 of them, appeared everywhere. In a practical touch the board of public works provided drinking fountains in his honour for every town. These bore the simple legend 'Trujillo provides water'. Even the Nigua insane asylum had a poster on its wall proclaiming 'We owe everything to Trujillo'. He ordered that his portrait appear alongside or instead of that of Christ in every house in the Dominican Republic and that he be referred to as the 'Godfather of the Nation'. He would, he announced, be prepared personally to baptize any child born during his presidency and proved as good as his word for the thousands of babies presented to him. Always prepared to please the public he then delighted them by ordering that the traditional Creole dance music, the *merengue*, become the national music of the Dominican Republic.

Yet Trujillo maintained a brutal regime that murdered

potential opponents while favouring his friends and family to an almost ludicrous degree – as when he made his seven-year-old son a colonel in the army and a general at the age of ten. He also gave himself grandiose titles such as 'First Journalist of the Republic', 'Genius of Peace', 'Protector of All Workers', 'Saviour of the Homeland' and 'Undefeated Generalissimo of the Dominican Armies'. Arrogantly he even arranged a campaign to nominate himself for the Nobel Peace Prize and his wife for the Nobel Literature Prize. Power had deprived him any sense of perspective. When he had come to power Trujillo had wasted no time in setting up a repressive dictatorship that in the customary tyrannical manner used a vast network of spies to eliminate potential opponents. His secret police used intimidation, torture and assassination to eliminate political opponents. The Dominican Republic was now his own personal kingdom as he continued to amass a personal fortune. For thirty-one years he ruled the country as president in 1930–8 and 1942–52. In the period when he was not in office he still retained absolute power while leaving the ceremonial affairs to puppet presidents such as his brother. Safe from outside political interference, courtesy of the USA, Trujillo's arrogance impelled him to start building himself a huge personality cult out of all proportion to his diminutive stature and the strategic importance of his country. Trujillo was known for his open-door policy, accepting Jewish refugees from Europe and Japanese migration during the 1930s. His arrogance towards the neighbouring country of Haiti led to aggressive policies, among them a uniquely Dominican policy of racial discrimination known as *Antihaitianismo* that targeted the mostly black inhabitants of his neighbouring country as well as those living along the Dominican borders.

His traditional allies including the Roman Catholic Church and members of the Dominican elite began turning against him. Most serious of all, the Eisenhower administration of the USA feared that Trujillo's ruthless suppression of dissent was leading to a radicalization of the Dominican rebels: this could lead to a full-scale revolution in the Dominican Republic similar to the one that had occurred in Fidel Castro's Cuba. To head off such an event the CIA began making contact with more conservative Dominican opposition. Events now moved to a violent conclusion, an assassination of the dictator accepted and aided by the CIA. A group of wealthy Dominicans with personal grudges against the dictator and whose families had suffered from Trujillo's arrogant reign carried out the deed. The CIA covertly supplied several carbine rifles for the assassins to slay Trujillo, and they promised US support for the new regime once the dictator was dead. On 30 May 1961 they assassinated Rafael Trujillo by ambushing his car outside the capital and shooting him dead.

Across the globe another dictator established a dictatorship with an even more flamboyant personality cult. In 1965 in the Central African Republic Jean-Bédel Bokassa, an ex-sergeant of the French colonial army, seized power. At first he attempted genuinely to improve the lot of the people in his poverty-stricken country only to give in to the temptations of self-aggrandizement. He began calling himself the 'Saviour of the Republic', 'Man of Steel' and 'Artist and Guide of Central Africa'. He introduced a revolutionary council with himself as its head. Then followed a series of measures intended to improve the moral climate of the nation, including the abolition of begging. He also revealed a deep obsession with France and French culture. His idol was Napoleon, and in 1976 he decided to make the Central African Republic a monarchy, with himself an emperor. He took the title of 'His Imperial Majesty the Emperor of Central Africa' and prepared for a lavish coronation modelled on that of his hero Napoleon Bonaparte. The cost was $20 million, but his French backers did not protest, and the lavish ceremony went ahead.

An international guest list was prepared and invitations sent around the world. Tons of exotic food and even ceremonial horses were imported from France. Trainee cavalrymen were sent to Europe to learn how to ride in the parade. The coronation had just about everything. It was perhaps the ultimate expression of political stagecraft and spectacle. Only one man benefited from one of the twentieth century's most decadent and outrageous celebrations. No world leaders of any consequence bothered to attend the ceremony, many already considering Bokassa insane and too similar in character to the dangerous Ugandan tyrant Idi Amin. All this was compounded by rumours that Bokassa ate human flesh. News of further atrocities led to his grip on power becoming ever more tenuous, and his 'empire' began to crumble. Finally his French paymasters withdrew their support, and when Bokassa ordered the arrest and brutal murder of protesting schoolchildren in January 1979 the French government ordered paratroopers to land and overthrow his regime. Bokassa himself retired into comfortable exile.

Although shrewder and more politically aware than Bokassa, Saddam Hussein of Iraq showed a similar arrogance and a compulsion to ignore the opinion of the outside world. Saddam played a dangerous game of provoking the most militarily powerful nation on Earth. His reign began, like so many other dictatorships, with an idealistic cause: that of promoting Pan-Arabism in the Middle East. He saw himself as the spiritual heir of President Nasser of Egypt and the new figurehead for uniting the Arabs. Saddam's opportunity came when the Iraqi monarchy established after the defeat of the Turks in the First World War was overthrown in 1958. The military junta that replaced it was led by General Abd al-Karim Qasim who five years later was murdered by a group of Sunni Ba'ath army officers that included Saddam. Arab morale was at a low ebb following the spectacular defeat by the Israelis in the 1967 war, but when Saddam became President of Iraq in 1979 he set about reviving the cause with the help of the Sunni minority. At first he seemed to justify the belief that artificially created countries like Iraq, with borders decided by international agreements after the First World War, work efficiently only under firm rule.

In spite of his professed high ideals, Iraq under Saddam soon became little more than another traditional tyranny run by the president and his cronies. The much-vaunted Ba'athist Party degenerated into a vehicle for corruption, while the country was rigidly controlled by Saddam's secret police, the Mukhabarat. Astute in his management of internal Iraqi politics Saddam was to prove catastrophically wrong when it came to foreign affairs. This was not surprising in a man who only briefly travelled outside Iraq during his life. His arrogant misjudgements when dealing with the USA and his immediate neighbours may well have been the result of this inexperience. The result was that he wrecked his country and fatally sabotaged his regime by the two invasions that he planned and executed – of Iran in 1980 and Kuwait in 1990. His high-handed assumption, in the case of Iran, was that American suspicions of Iran would be enough for him to be given tacit backing by the USA. After all, he later recalled, a joint front against Iran had been the basis of Iraqi–American cooperation in the 1980s. The ill-judged attempt to annex oil-rich Kuwait followed and led to the destruction of a large part of his military capability. The US failure to press home their advantage, invade Iraq and impose regime change gave Saddam a second chance. This he wasted by indulging in a dangerous game of cat and mouse with the USA over the issue of weapons of mass destruction. His refusal to answer the question of whether or not he possessed the notorious weapons led eventually to invasion by the USA and its allies and Saddam's overthrow and death.

Saddam Hussein showed all the arrogance of an angry, destructive personality. He was prepared to allow Baghdad to be destroyed rather than surrender to the massively overwhelming military might of the USA and the coalition forces. Saddam's justification was that Iraq could never appear weak in front of its local enemies, especially Iran. This is the explanation he gave for keeping the world guessing whether he had weapons of mass destruction. Saddam Hussein's failing was not stupidity but arrogance. He was a man of intelligence who came to believe that he had semi-divine attributes. Even at his trial after he was captured he refused to alter his attitude. As Alice Weiser, a graphologist who gave evidence about Saddam's body language, said, 'His demeanor to me shows . . . [that he's] arrogant, combative, controlling, when he points with his fist, it's intimidating and it's arrogant, and when you continue to do that – at one point he used two fists to point – that's double defiance and rebelliousness and pointing the guilt at you . . . As far as he's concerned, he's very much in control.'

10
A PRETENSION OF CREATIVITY

O ne of the well-known facts about Adolf Hitler's early life is that he wanted to an artist but failed. Had he been allowed to study art as he wished, it has been argued, the world might well have been spared the horrors of his political career, a world war and the Holocaust. Instead, twice rejected by the Kunstgewerbeschule, Vienna's leading art school, in 1907 and 1908 he sank into depression and resentment against a society that had refused to recognize his genius. Ironically the few pictures he managed to sell in Vienna were bought by Jews. His obsession with art was now channelled into a fanatical interest in politics. A corrupt hierarchy had, as far as Hitler was concerned, stopped him becoming a great painter like his contemporary, Oskar Kokoschka, soon to become the most famous Austrian painter of his generation. What made it worse for Hitler was that while Kokoschka foisted modern and degenerate art on the world, Hitler would have remained true to the classical tradition. It was not just Hitler's loss but the art world's loss. Hitler's unshakeable belief in his own cultural judgement is not unique among tyrants for it has been a characteristic of these despots since history began. For such men control of cultural life is a natural extension of control over the political and social life of a nation. Like Hitler they have thought themselves to be artistically gifted or shown a keen and interfering interest in their national culture, none more so than the Roman Emperor Nero.

As a young man Nero appeared to be an artistically gifted and was encouraged by his tutors to study poetry, drama, sculpture and painting. His intelligence was apparent to all those around him, and he would frequently dine with the leading poets and artists of the day – not that any could refuse such an invitation from the tyrannical ruler. These parties later included many of Rome's leading philosophers, such as Seneca, who was called upon to discuss moral issues with the future emperor. Talented in his own opinion in every branch of the arts, Nero reserved his greatest passion for music. Nor was he a mere dilettante in his approach to achieving musical success. Not only did he practise enthusiastically as a singer but he was prepared to exercise daily with heavy lead weights on his chest to strengthen his diaphragm. With these rigorous exercises went a special diet and the use of purgatives to improve his performance. Pliny the Elder reported that on certain days Nero ate only a dish of chives in olive oil in order to sweeten the tone of his voice. Yet Nero saw himself not only as a gifted singer but also as a talented player of the cithara, a musical instrument like a lyre. This he insisted on playing, to public dismay, at Rome's Juvenilia games, which he had founded in AD 59.

In Ancient Rome sport ranked alongside music and poetry as an essential part of cultural life, and Nero was determined to play his full part in this, too. His chosen sport was chariot racing, and he entered contests with a win-at-all-costs determination. He not only won the chariot race despite falling out of his chariot but also introduced several new events of a musical nature. The judges prudently declared him the winner of them all. Flushed with success, he made the rounds of the Isthmian, Nemean, Pythian and Panathean Games and handsomely won numerous events at every one. During his performances nobody was allowed to leave, although a few people got round that by feigning death and being carried out. These games were not usually all held in the same year, but in AD 67 they made an exception for Nero because his offer was just too good to refuse. He returned to Rome, a tired but happy emperor, with 1,800 prizes. Normally these would have been wreaths of laurel or bay that an athlete could take home to his wife for the stock pot, but so overwhelmed were his loyal subjects by Nero's talent that they made another exception and presented him with jewels and precious objects. A dedicated Hellenist, he deeply admired Greek culture and attempted to revive the Olympic games in Rome. Their appeal was that the Greek games combined physical prowess with artistic endeavour: as well as competing in athletics, young men tested their skills against each other in oratory, poetry, singing and instrument-playing.

As might be expected, Nero considered himself no less proficient a writer and dramatist than he was an exponent of the other arts. He proved a generous patron of writers and poets in what became known as the age of Silver Latin. He offered financial support to young poets and encouraged members of his entourage to do the same. Among those who enjoyed his patrimony was Gaius Petronius, whose *Satyricon* mocks the golden decadence of Nero's court. Although his predecessors Augustus and Tiberius had written poetry in both Latin and Greek, Nero far surpassed them in ability. As competitive in the arts as he was in sport he was determined to win first prize in every poetry competition that he entered. Whenever he competed he was invariably the winner for few judges were bold enough to deprive him of victory. One of his greatest triumphs was to perform in Greek at a poetry competition in Naples in AD 64. Some Alexandrians present applauded him with rhythmic clapping that so impressed Nero that he ordered Roman audiences to do the same in future. 'The Greeks alone know how to appreciate me and my art,' he confided to one of his attendants.

Shortly before his death Nero set out, like a present-day rock star, on a farewell recital tour of Italy and Greece. He arrived back in Rome dressed in a Greek cloak and wearing an Olympic crown that he had been allowed to win. He rode through the Augustan Gate without the customary military trappings of an emperor. Instead he returned in artistic triumph proceeded by the laurel crowns awarded for artistic triumphs borne by actors and musicians. Throughout his life he remained obsessed by the arts and far more interested in culture than in ruling. Among subsequent rulers, King Ludwig II of Bavaria in the nineteenth century was as dedicated as Nero to art and architecture, being the patron of Wagner and the builder of equally exotic palaces. Appropriately as he awaited assassination his main concern was for his reputation as an artist and performer. He began preparing himself for suicide, then, losing his nerve, he first begged for one of his companions to set an example by first killing himself. At last the sound of approaching horsemen drove Nero to face the end. However, he still could not bring himself to take his own life, so instead he forced his private secretary, Epaphroditos, to perform the task. Nero's famous dying words were 'What an artist dies in me.'

Every modern dictator has been acutely aware that apart from his personal artistic predilections control of the national culture was a prerequisite for control of the people. What is fascinating is just how seriously totalitarian regimes took the issue and how closely each despot became involved. All three leading totalitarian regimes of the twentieth century – Nazi Germany, Soviet Russia and Fascist Italy – shared an obsession with grandiose architectural projects, large-scale pageants and the elevation of early 'folk' art to the position of a national culture.

Hitler's own obsessive involvement was typical of this process. After his failure to enter the Kunstgewerbeschule in Vienna he blamed his rejection on everyone but himself; it was the fault of the teachers who had failed to prepare him properly for the examination; it was due to the fact that he was the archetypal outsider in Prussian-dominated German society. What is known of his schooldays in the provincial Austrian town of Linz is that he was mocked by other boys as a country bumpkin. His teachers had no higher opinion of him, dismissing him as a poor scholar who objected to having to learn French. One teacher thought him the most sulky boy that he had ever taught. Lazy and resentful, the young Adolf Hitler finally attributed his failure not to himself but to the evil influence of the Jews on German education. So began his obsession with the baleful influence of Jews on German art and education. Yet not a single member of the Kunstgewer-beschule committee that rejected him was Jewish. Moreover the only person in Vienna who continued to buy his paintings was Samuel Morgenstern, a Jew. For some reason the dull, grim landscape watercolours that Hitler produced appealed to Morgenstern. They appear in complete contrast to the dynamic and progressive work being produced by other German artists. Given Hitler's obsessive resentments it was not long before he conceived of a particular hatred for the person and works of his fellow Austrian Oskar Kokoschka and the adventurous canvases of Wassily Kandinsky, Paul Klee and George Grosz.

Once formed Hitler's tastes were as unshakeable as his prejudices, and his favourite painter remained Adolf Ziegler, a man known mockingly in the Renaissance manner as the 'Master of the German pubic hair' for his leaden studies of monumental naked Nazi storm troopers and their blonde maidens. Hitler's artistic tastes offer an important insight into his personality. As the psychoanalyst Alice Miller has suggested 'Hitler's total rejection of modernism implies a rejection of colour; and colour is important because it stands for emotions, which represent a dangerous threat to a person like Hitler. The vague and imprecise lines used in modern drawing were almost as bad as splashes of colour – both were a threat that could lead to loss of control.'

Hitler ensured that his own prejudices were shared by his fellow leading Nazis and encouraged a crusade to rid pure, traditional German art of such international contamination. This in turn led to the infamous exhibition of so-called 'degenerate' art, the 'Entartete Kunst', which opened in Munich in 1937 and toured every major German city. Hans Hinkel, Hitler's chief cultural adviser, said at the time, 'Hand any of these paintings to an

ordinary worker and he couldn't tell the top from the bottom . . .
art for the experts is not art . . . a new German art must be created
for the people.' Hitler was delighted with the exhibition,
declaring that in future German art must only reflect the eternal
truths of beauty and not be the subject of transitory fashion. Most
importantly German art must be national in its subject matter and
totally devoid of any Jewish taint. Yet only six of the one hundred
artists mocked in the Entartete Kunst were actually Jewish. To the
Nazis' initial delight more than 3 million people flocked to the
exhibition; either Hitler was right and the German people shared
his taste in art, or they came to take a last look at some of
Germany's most important modern paintings. The matter was
resolved to Hitler's embarrassment when a second exhibition of
Nazi approved art toured the country. It attracted less than one-
fifth of the audience that had attended the Entarte Kunst.

Hitler thought himself as much an arbiter of architectural
taste as he was of painting. Again it was an ossified traditionalism
that prevailed, encouraged by the conservative new buildings that
had arisen in Austria and Germany during his youth. This neo-
Baroque architecture that appeared under Kaiser Wilhelm II and
buildings in the style of Classical Romanticism suited him
perfectly. Either style could be used as the physical statements of
the new Nazi regime and its emphasis on 'blood and soil'. The
man best suited to bringing Hitler's architectural dream to life was
Albert Speer who belonged to a generation of young professionals
born between 1900 and 1910 and who had experienced the First
World War as children or adolescents. Later they advanced to key
executive positions in the new regime – a young expert elite, often
highly ambitious and competitive but with little empathy for the
suffering of others. A frustrated architect himself, the Führer saw
in Speer a means of fulfilling his own youthful dreams. Writer
Gitta Sereny has claimed that Hitler and Speer were attracted
to each other because of their psychological past; she describes
their relationship as follows: 'Both were bedevilled from child-

hood by thwarted, imagined and withheld love, a deficiency which rendered them both virtually incapable of expressing private emotions ... Both of them, capable of great charm and courted by women, could barely respond though neither of them was homosexual.'

When Speer set to work he avoided this traditional neo-Baroque style in favour of his own version of 1930s Modernism. Oddly Speer chose to ignore the modern construction methods of steel and reinforced concrete that had been used in Fascist Italy. Instead he pleased Hitler by choosing such historic materials as stone to provide his buildings with a monumental timelessness. Speer wrote in his memoirs that, 'The Romans built arches of triumph to celebrate the big victories won by the Roman Empire, while Hitler built them to celebrate victories he had not yet won.' Yet there is another psychological explanation for Hitler's obsession with architecture and his passion for constructing huge buildings, stadia, bridges and motorways. They could be seen as an attempt to compensate for his lack of confidence – tangible proofs of his greatness, designed to impress himself as much as others. In his own eyes he was the greatest man in the world; therefore he needed to build the greatest and largest of everything. He regarded most of the structures he erected as temporary buildings on a par with ordinary mortals; the permanent buildings he planned to construct later. They would be much larger and grander – designed to last a thousand years. In other words, they would be fitting monuments to him. It has also been suggested that the frequency with which gigantic pillars appear in his buildings is significant and these architectural erections can be seen as phallic symbols and an unconscious attempt to compensate for his own impotence.

As traditional as Hitler's cultural preferences were he was prepared to delegate control of the cultural life of the German people to one man, his minister of propaganda, Joseph Goebbels. In this Goebbels proved himself a genius of communications and largely responsible for establishing the system of biased information without which any modern government cannot function, whether it be a democracy or not. Goebbels masterfully promoted the image of Hitler as the Messiah-redeemer who had come to save the soul of Germany. His weapon was the total control of the media of the time. The relatively new radio service – along with the press, publishing, cinema and the arts – was ruthlessly annexed to promote the vision of a new Nazi cultural life. Competing ideas were eradicated, as were all freedoms of expression that disappeared from German cultural life. The first to go were any positive mention of the Jews, socialists or other political opponents. Goebbels then celebrated his success with a notorious event that came to symbolize the nihilism of Nazi culture. On 10 May 1933 outside the Berlin Opera House more than 25,000 volumes of 'un-German' books by Jewish and left-wing authors (including the works of two of German's greatest living writers, Bertholt Brecht and Thomas Mann) were publicly burned by SS storm troopers and Nazi students. As Mann said later in exile in America, 'They were burning books that they were incapable of writing.'

While Hitler sought to obliterate contemporary German culture Joseph Stalin was providing Soviet Russia with the benefit of his own cultural genius. Stalin, too, considered himself the sole arbiter of artistic taste for an entire nation. Arguably the best-educated tyrant since Nero, Stalin was not inhibited in declaring his opinions. His self-confidence resulted from the excellent teaching he had received at a religious seminary in Georgia, where his mother had sent him in the hope that he would become an Orthodox priest. Unlike Hitler, Stalin had worked hard at his study. His broad knowledge included not only politics and history but also Georgian, Russian and Classical Greek literature. He had written poetry, too: the strange, cold images of his verse are an indication of his later isolation when in power. Later his library at the Kremlin contained more than 20,000 volumes; he was known to read avidly every day whenever time allowed. Each new book would be personally annotated with his thoughts and comments. Not that his broad reading instilled much human empathy in him. Some of Stalin's reading material is surprising; during the General Strike in Britain in 1926 he became fascinated with British history and started to learn English. Cunningly he always kept this knowledge to himself and never revealed his secret erudition to those around him and sought to give the impression that he knew far less than he really did.

Stalin's control of Soviet culture, particularly music and cinematography, was infamous. In general he followed the Leninist tradition by which culture celebrated a united workforce and selfless dedication to the state. With this went an emphasis on good health and a commitment to strong family values. For Stalin this meant maintaining strict censorship of the arts and banning all romantic freethinking and politically incorrect ideas. His ethos was high seriousness more concerned with economic self-improvement than social ideas. Soviet Russia under Stalin was above all a serious society committed to economic rather than social progress. The Soviet state had no time for cultural ephemera; anything that was thought too light-hearted was simply banned – and that included detective stories, romances and even comic books. The cultural life of the Soviet Union became as conformist as its orthodox politics. There was no conflict of ideas, only the petty disputes between the conformist artists as they vied with each other for state patronage.

What most alarmed Stalin, the cultural tsar, was the prospect of a return to the cultural near-anarchy that existed before the fall of Trotsky in 1928. Then such groups as the Revolutionary Association of Proletarian Writers were bold enough to encourage their members openly to criticize faults in the system. Many thought that rather than threatening the regime, such articles added credibility and could only lead to improvements that would make the Soviet Union an even more formidable foe to the corrupt and outdated free world. For the radical ideas of communism to continue to flourish there must be a degree of artistic freedom. Unfortunately, driven by his own paranoia, Stalin could not agree. He viewed all cultural expression, whether from the left or right, with equal suspicion. The state must exercise complete cultural control or everything would be lost. For this reason and soon after he came to power in 1924 he banned all Russia's most prominent artists and composers from showing their work in public without his own specific approval.

One of the greatest sufferers was the composer Dmitri Shostakovich, who found it difficult to predict how Stalin would react to each of his new works. For Shostakovich, each première became a nail-biting experience. One of the worst was in 1936, when at the prèmiere of Shostakovich's new opera *Lady Macbeth of Mtsensk* Stalin was seen to sulk in his seat, an undisguised sneer of contempt on his face. Clearly he was shocked by the radical opera and its discordant music. The following day Shostakovich, on direct or indirect orders from Stalin, was roundly attacked in *Pravda* for having composed a 'muddle instead of music'. Shostakovich claims that from that day until the death of Stalin he was in mortal fear of his life – aware that he could be arrested and eliminated at any time.

Stalin knew little about the technicalities of music but knew what he liked or rather what he did not like. Where filmmaking was concerned he prided himself on being something of a technical expert. He also fully believed in Lenin's dictum that 'For us the cinema is the most important of the arts.' The new medium had as much appeal for Stalin as it had for Goebbels, and he shared the German propagandist's view that cinema would become the cultural bulwark of the new state. The archives show that Stalin bombarded Soviet filmmakers with suggestions for projects as well as attempting to get involved in projects already in production. He acted in many ways like a capitalist Hollywood studio boss. An avid viewer, he watched new films after dinner in the Kremlin whenever possible. If they were Russian productions the directors waited nervously in another room for Stalin's first reactions. When Berlin fell to the Russian in 1945 Stalin made sure that he acquired Joseph Goebbels's own film library and was amused to discover that they had the same taste in Hollywood classics. Both liked Charlie Chaplin films, Hollywood comedies and *Tarzan, the Ape Man*. Stalin's favourite Western star was surprisingly, John Wayne although he was often scathing about Wayne's well-known anti-communism, once telling Nikita Khrushchev that someone ought to assassinate him just to shut him up.

If anything Stalin's obsession with films and filmmaking grew over the years. Even the great film director Sergei Eisenstein would be summoned to the Kremlin to discuss the finer points of a production. Eisenstein had just begun editing *Alexander Nevsky*, the epic story of Russian infantry defeating mounted German knights in the thirteenth century, when he was ordered to the Kremlin. Stalin told him flatly that from what he had already seen Eisenstein must immediately re-edit the battle scenes. The Soviet Union was in the process of negotiating the infamous non-aggression pact with Germany. Scenes of German soldiers being humiliated on the battlefield would therefore be inappropriate and embarrassing. Eisenstein had little option but to agree and make the changes that Stalin demanded. Wary of offending the despot a second time, Eisenstein submitted the entire script to Stalin of his two-part film *Ivan the Terrible* in 1944 for approval. Each scene was then discussed in great detail, with the director being told revealingly, 'Yes, Ivan was very cruel. You can show that he was cruel. But you must also show the reasons for his cruelty.' Even when given permission to proceed Eisenstein remained apprehensive of Stalin's reaction. When Part One was completed, Eisenstein lost his nerve and made Part Two so anodyne that Stalin was offended by his treatment and dismissed the work as 'some kind of nightmare', making sure that film was immediately banned.

Stalin's grip on the cultural life of the Soviet Union was remorseless in architecture, too. Everything had to conform to the essential task of promoting the Soviet Union as the world's dominant communist state. For this reason he favoured public over private space, and the open spaces in every Soviet city became decorated with monumental buildings. Often historic buildings were swept aside to make way for the new civic leviathans that came to characterize the post-war Moscow skyline. Fortunately plans for a 380-metre-high (1,250-foot) tower surmounted by a massive statue of Lenin were abandoned, although the historic Church of Christ the Saviour in central Moscow had already been demolished to make way for it. It was not buildings but the Moscow metro – with its spacious stations clad in marble and decorated with huge glass chandeliers – that came to commemorate Stalin's era of Soviet Classicism.

Although he maintained a close watch on the cultural output of the Soviet Union throughout the 1930s Stalin was careful at that time to keep a low profile himself. This changed in 1945 after the spectacular victory of the Soviet Union over Nazi Germany. Stalin now felt confident enough to emerge from the shadows and play a full role in the joyful celebrations that broke out throughout the nation. The heroism of the Soviet people was celebrated in all branches of the arts, and Stalin himself was portrayed as the driving force that had saved the nation from disaster. This version of events was wholeheartedly accepted by the rest of the world, too. As yet there was little international awareness of his terrible crimes against his own people. The image of Joseph Stain as the avuncular face of world communism was eagerly accepted. Comrade Stalin was now an acceptable world figure, idolized by communist sympathizers everywhere and with a leaden grip on Soviet culture. The triumph of Stain was also the triumph of Socialist Realism. Anyone who attempted to deviate – such as the writers Osip Mandelstam, Isaac Babel and Boris Pilnyak – were imprisoned, killed or died of starvation in the gulags. A handful of exiled dissidents, including Boris Pasternak, first alerted the world to Stalin's appalling abuse of human rights and the arts.

The third great totalitarian ruler of the twentieth century, Mao Tse-tung, was equally obsessed with imposing his own particular idea of culture on his people. For Mao's China, monumental architecture was not possible because the nation had neither the necessary resources nor a building industry capable of undertaking monumental architecture. When he came to power in 1949 Mao was at first happy to leave the artists, writers and composers to themselves, but by 1966, when the first impetus of the revolution had ended, he saw the need to do something more radical to motivate the people. He wrote, 'Our literary and art workers must accomplish this task and shift their stand; they must gradually move their feet over to the side of the workers, peasants and soldiers, to the side of the proletariat, through the process of going into their very midst and into the thick of practical struggles and through the process of studying Marxism and society. Only in this way can we have a literature and art that are truly for the workers, peasants and soldiers, a truly proletarian literature and art.' Mao was convinced that it was the nation's moribund educational system that was holding back progress. Only a comprehensive reform of education and culture would bring a new intellectual life to the country. This led to the idea of a Cultural Revolution. It was also Mao's response to a growing challenge for power that was becoming evident among some of his closest supporters who opposed to the growing influence of his wife, Jiang Qing, and the favouritism shown to some members of his regime.

The Cultural Revolution began in August 1966 when with government encouragement a group of high-school girls began demonstrating on the streets of Beijing. Their actions sparked a series of nationwide demonstrations and near-riots by the young.

Mao, as he hoped, was seen as the spiritual leader of the movement, and his *Little Red Book* became its bible. Published two years earlier, the book became one of the most influential publications in history, selling more than 900 million copies. The *LRB* was essential reading for every Chinese citizen, and being without a copy invited a beating in the streets. Students chanting passages from it thronged the streets of all the major Chinese cities. This new orthodoxy was enforced by the quasi-military 'Red Guards' who were given free railway passes to spread Mao's ideas all over the country. Mao's clandestine opponents were driven from office – only Deng Xiaoping managing to survive the purge to later emerge as the leader of a post-Mao China. The first targets of the Red Guards included Buddhist temples, churches and mosques, which were razed to the ground or converted to other uses. Sacred texts, as well as Confucian writings, were burned, along with religious statues and other artwork. Any object associated with China's pre-revolutionary past was liable to be destroyed. In their fervour the Red Guards began to persecute people deemed 'counter-revolutionary' or 'bourgeois', as well. The Guards conducted so-called 'struggle sessions' in which they heaped abuse and public humiliation upon people accused of capitalist thoughts – such as teachers, monks and other educated persons. These sessions often included physical violence, and many of the accused died or ended up being held in re-education camps for years.

By February 1967 China had descended into chaos. The purges had reached the level of army generals who dared to speak out against the excesses of the Cultural Revolution, and groups of Red Guards were turning against one another and fighting in the streets. Mao's wife, Jiang Qing, encouraged the Red Guards to raid arms from the People's Liberation Army and even to replace the army entirely if necessary. By December 1968 even Mao realized that the Cultural Revolution was spinning out of control. China's economy, already weakened by the Great Leap Forward, was faltering badly. Industrial production fell by 12 per cent in just two years. In reaction Mao issued a call for the 'Down to the Countryside Movement', a chilling precursor of what Pol Pot would later carry out in Cambodia. Young cadres from the city were sent to live on farms and learn from the peasants. Although he spun this idea as a tool for levelling society in fact Mao sought to disperse the Red Guards across the country so that they could not cause so much trouble any more. This was to prove the turning point of the Cultural Revolution as the more excessive behaviour of the Guards was brought under control. By then more than two-thirds of the old Central Committee had been driven from office and the economy stagnated. Rather than improving Chinese cultural education the Cultural Revolution had virtually destroyed it – a whole generation had lost the chance of proper schooling and a university education. Mao's attempt to hang on to power by encouraging mob tactics against some of the most important traditions in Chinese culture had proved a near-disaster.

11
MANIC BEHAVIOUR

Emperor Caligula behaved with a strange hostility to those around him that eventually took the form of sadism. Some have attributed this to his resentment against those he blamed for the death of his father, Germanicus – above all, Emperor Tiberius who some thought had induced his agent, Piso, to poison Germanicus. Caligula's mother, Agrippina the Elder, shared his suspicions and made this so apparent that Tiberius quickly came up with a solution to be rid of her and to silence her: he had her tried for treason and then banished to Pandataria (modern Ventotene), an island off the Campanian coast where she eventually died of starvation.

Caligula's sadism, which led him to persecute his own senators, may have had its roots in the misery of his childhood on Capri when in the clutches of Tiberius, as well as his later bout of mental illness. With this emotional damage, constant insomnia and an epileptic condition it is clear that Caligula was plagued with many mental problems during his childhood that would follow him into adulthood. His later psychotic behaviour as Roman emperor further revealed the psychological damage that had been done during the course of his traumatic life. Most historians generally describe his rule as a period of scandalous insanity – and rightfully so. No wonder elements of Caligula's madness during his reign were reflected in violent unpredictability, sexual promiscuity and crude social behaviour towards his peers. His was intolerable behaviour, even for an emperor, as a plot to be rid of him was soon formed.

In January AD 41, members of the Praetorian Guard stabbed him to death as he walked from his apartments. The leader was

Cassius Chaerea, a man Caligula had once mocked for effeminacy in front of the whole court. Many different theories have been produced to explain Caligula's manic and sadistic behaviour. One suggestion was that an illness he had in AD 37 was bacterial meningitis and that this left residual mental defects. Another theory is that the illness, described by contemporaries as a mental breakdown, was a first attack of epilepsy. It is known that changes of mood characterized by surliness and irritability may precede an attack for an epileptic. In these epileptic psychoses there may be hallucinations, great fear and, sometimes, religious ecstasy. A more persistent theory is that Caligula suffered from encephalitis, which was not uncommon at the time. What is certain is that during the later years of his reign and after some mysterious illness that he suffered at the age of twenty-five, he showed undoubted mental derangement characterized by self-deification, sadism, perversion, great extravagance and vivid dreams.

After Caligula's death Rome did not have to wait long for another emperor of doubtful sanity to take the throne. The very name of Nero has become synonymous with sadism; as the nephew of Caligula he may have inherited the mental instability of his uncle. Yet eyewitness accounts of his odd behaviour indicate that he was more likely to have been a masochist. The writer Petronius, a close witness of the emperor's lifestyle, mocked life at Nero's court in his famous work the *Satyricon*, claiming 'it was more useful to use one's genitals than one's genius'. According to Petronius, the whole court was suffused with sadomasochism. Nero was deferential to strong figures including his mother Agrippina and his tutor Seneca; he was even seen to be subservient on occasion to his guard commander Burrus. He was known to go out at night dressed as a slave and to return the following morning with his face bruised. When he played stage roles he often chose submissive characters – such as a man in chains – or roles that involved transvestism, such a bride being made love to by her husband.

Nero's obvious masochism may have prompted his strange behaviour in dramatic competitions, as he always pretended to be at the mercy of the judges, falling on his knees in supplication. Why an emperor would need to do this – particularly as he persistently bribed up to 5,000 people to come along and applaud him – remains a mystery. In AD 68 Nero appears to have indulged in the ultimate act of masochism. When warned that his enemies were coming to kill him he refused to escape or even summon his guards. Instead he remained quietly at the palace and ordered his servants to dig him a grave in the grounds. When the assassins arrived he asked his most trusted attendant to help him cut his own throat. Insane or not, Nero was certainly one of the most charismatic figures in the whole of Roman history. Long after he was declared dead the people refused to believe it and at least three Nero impostors appeared, claiming to be the lost emperor. The most convincing not only looked like him but also seemed to have all Nero's old skills such as a good singing voice and an ability to play the cithara. A decade later another cithara-playing Nero emerged in Asia and led a rebellion that was put down with some difficulty by the legions. Yet the cult of the lost emperor remained; in AD 422, almost 400 years after his death, St Augustine of Hippo, disgusted by Nero's lingering admirers, wrote that 'Some suppose that he is not even dead . . . that he now lives in concealment and will live until he is revealed in his own time and restored to his kingdom.'

Apart from Caligula and Nero many tyrants have shown symptoms of manic behaviour but none as comprehensively as Vlad Tepes, the ruler of Wallachia in the fifteenth century. That he has become known as Vlad the Impaler shows his reputation for unusual and manic cruelty. Held hostage as a child by the Ottoman Turks Vlad was eventually released and returned to Wallachia as sovereign in 1448. His childhood humiliation as a prisoner was to fuel a quest for revenge on his childhood tormentors and led to his bitter campaign against his Turkish overlords. Matters were not helped by his brother Radu's decision to remain at the sultan's court with the hated enemy. On arrival in Wallachia Vlad discovered that his father had been assassinated a year earlier – buried alive by his own rebellious boyar nobles. Before this the same fate had been meted out to his eldest brother; other boyars had burned out his eyes with hot stakes before also burying him alive. Vlad's subsequent attack on boyar power was therefore as inevitable as that of his disciple Ivan the Terrible a century later.

Although he was ruler of Wallachia for just seven years Vlad's demonic energy was such that he became one of the most notorious tyrants in Eastern European history. His onslaught on his Turkish enemies was only equalled by the revenge he took on his own treacherous boyars. The viciousness of Vlad's methods shocked his enemies so that the number of infractions by his enemies soon decreased. At that time there were more methods of torturing or punishing a delinquent by death but Vlad became notorious for one of the most terrible executions – by impaling. His penchant for impaling his enemies on stakes in the ground and leaving them to die earned him his name Vlad the Impaler. He inflicted this type of torture on foreign and domestic enemies alike: notably as he retreated from a battle in 1462 he left a field filled with thousands of impaled victims as a deterrent to pursuing Ottoman forces. Vlad's ruthlessness was unqualified; he employed every possible means to gain an advantage: drawing the enemy deep into his own territory through a strategic retreat he burned villages and poisoned wells along the route; he employed guerrilla tactics, using the local terrain to advantage; he even initiated a form of germ warfare, deliberately sending victims of infectious diseases into the Turkish camps. The historical documents that survive portray Vlad as a psychopathic tyrant while at the same time praising him as a national hero who was forced to use ruthless methods against a pitiless foe. Tales of Vlad's exploits against the Ottomans circulated throughout Christian Europe in the fifteenth century, earning him both fear and respect. Mostly written in German they were illustrated with woodcuts that depicted in detail the despot and his atrocities. Vlad's name will for ever be associated with manic sadism, but he is also remembered for standing up against the Ottoman Empire at a time when other principalities around him were falling under Turkish control. He is perceived as something of a David facing a Goliath. As for the brutality of his punishments his defenders point out that his actions were no more cruel than those of several other late-medieval or early Renaissance European rulers such as Louis XI of France, Ferdinand I of Naples, Cesare Borgia of Italy and Ivan the Terrible of Russia.

As vicious as Vlad had been few have questioned his sanity. But when considering the behaviour of Ivan the Terrible of Russia it is almost impossible not to believe that he was clinically insane. At the very least he appears to have spent large parts of his life drifting in and out of bouts of insanity. Ivan was certainly paranoid about his health – as seen in his recorded morbid anxiety about himself. He was also convinced that he was the victim of conspiracies and that there were constant plots to poison him. Unstable from an early age he suddenly in 1553 suffered a more fundamental breakdown in his mental health. He appeared to have developed a fever, perhaps caused by pneumonia or even encephalitis. Those around him realized the seriousness of his condition as he drifted in and out of consciousness in the Kremlin. At one point death seemed inevitable as he summoned the leading boyars to his bedside and ordered that on his death they all swear an immediate oath of allegiance to his six-month-old son and heir, Dmitry. With the likely death of the tsar imminent the boyars were in confusion: some obeyed, but others either ignored Ivan's appeal or left the palace. Ivan recovered, but the experience of the anarchy that had occurred marked his behaviour for the rest of his life. From that moment his latent paranoia erupted into a constant suspicion of those around him and the fear that he would soon be assassinated.

His terror of poisoning was intensified seven years later when his beloved wife Anastasia was taken suddenly ill and died. As she was borne to the grave Ivan followed her bier wailing and moaning in a manic manner and calling out that his enemies had killed his innocent spouse with magic or poison. Anastasia had been the only person he appeared to trust. With her death Ivan must have felt as isolated as he had been as a child at a hostile court surrounded by dangerous enemies. The emotional damage done by his illness now intensified as his behaviour became ever more manic. The harsh cruelty and erratic behaviour intensified and was exacerbated by sudden bouts of inexplicable rage. Violent mood swings followed ever-wilder bouts of drinking, fornication and sodomy. His friends were urged to join him in carnival-like excesses. Without the heavy drinking he appeared to be emulating the behaviour of Vlad the Impaler a century earlier. It has even been suggested that Ivan as a child may have read accounts of Vlad that presented him as a hero-king and this inspired Ivan to emulate the Wallachian despot when he came to the Russian throne. There are certainly some striking similarities between them, such as the need to chastise the arrogant nobles who surrounded them. There was also the necessity to be wary of the threat of foreign invasion. The difference was Ivan's certainty that he had been sent to do God's work, and that he ruled Russia by divine right. 'I am subject to no one except Christ, Son of God,' he stated unequivocally. Therefore he had no need to explain his war of revenge on the boyars or the punishment handed out to anyone who opposed his will. To question his motives, therefore, would be to oppose God – and anyone who did it would deserve their fate. For Ivan using violence against dissenters became a sacred duty and cruelty a means of purification. Only in Spain at the height of the Holy Inquisition would such an argument, that these actions were inspired and driven by God himself, seem plausible.

Ivan's image of himself as the vengeful tsar seemed appropriate to the Russian need for a powerful and father-like ruler who had the right to punish evil and those who strayed from the path of righteousness. Ivan was confident that this was indeed true and claimed as much in a letter to his childhood friend and adviser Prince Andrey Kurbsky. He asked Kurbsky why, if he was so righteous and pious, he did not 'willingly accept . . . suffering from me, your master, and so inherit the crown of life?' The greatest single act of supposed divine punishment was Ivan's destruction of the city of Novgorod in January 1570. This was done because Ivan suspected that its citizens were planning to hand it over to the approaching Poles. Ivan commanded a second wall to be built around the city and began an attack. On every subsequent day the Russian troops killed up to a thousand defenders in battle and any prisoners were taken and tortured to death in the presence of Ivan and his son. Only after 20,000 of its citizens had been killed or died of starvation did Novgorod finally surrender.

As his mania increased Ivan suffered frequent dramatic mood swings, culminating shortly before Christmas 1564 in his announcing to the court that he had decided to give up the throne of Russia and retire to the country. As the boyars discussed what to do Ivan's treasures were packed on to carts and he left Moscow. This may well have been a cunning ploy to flush out conspirators who would then make an attempt on the throne. Yet nothing happened, leaving the throne unoccupied. Then according to court records the Russian people began to clamour for the tsar's return. Ivan might well have seen this as an opportunity to return and rule on his own terms, and after careful negotiations he agreed, but on the condition that the people accept he had the right to rule without any conditions or interference. What had appeared an act of lunacy on Ivan's part was in reality a cunning move to gain unfettered power. That moment unleashed a reign of terror. Now armed with supreme power Ivan returned in triumph to Moscow and set about teaching the boyars a bitter lesson. Soon the men who had poisoned his childhood were being subjected to an implacable revenge. Arrested on the least suspicion or on the word of the many informers that thronged his court they were subjected to the most appalling cruelties. New and even more sadistic methods of torture were introduced. Scenes of torment worthy of the paintings of Hieronymus Bosch were enacted in real life with one suspect noble impaled on a stake and taking fifteen hours to die in agony. When the victim's mother came to pray for her dying son, Ivan ordered his men to rape and kill her and then fed her remains to his hunting dogs.

Seldom in history has such cruelty been administered by a ruler anywhere in the world. Yet armed with his mandate from the people, Ivan claimed that he was cleansing the world of sinners. It is clear that the long and protracted tortures and the keen personal interest he took in the tortures and lingering deaths of his enemies show that his claims of revenge were merely a cover for the indulgence of his innate sadism. Russia suffered morally but also economically as Ivan imposed ever more crippling taxes that harmed trade. The revenue raised was then used fund more military campaigns as the country declined into ruin with abandoned farms and depopulated villages.

There is little doubt that Ivan the Terrible was a malevolent psychopath of the most dangerous kind. Such men are vindictive and have a tendency to believe that any display of goodwill by individuals is a plot aimed at deceiving them. Most cases of murder are committed by these types of psychopaths since they tend to be fearless and lack feelings of guilt for their actions. The tyrannical psychopaths tend to be frightening because the weaknesses of others trigger them into becoming intimidators, and this offers them a chance of attacking the weak. They take pleasure in seeing the agony that people go through as a result of the pain that the psychopaths have inflicted on them. These types are driven into violent acts because of the fear they have that other individuals will identify their inner insecurities; at the same time they usually have a serious case of low self-esteem – although it is difficult to see this in Ivan the Terrible.

The terror continued with his subjects being randomly tortured, robbed or raped – often merely to provide the tsar with sadistic entertainment. Friendships meant little him and being close to the tsar carried the risk of sudden arrest and execution. Ivan continued to be wracked by guilt, not for the atrocities he was committing but for the supposed religious sins of blasphemy and fornication. He had now taken the divine right of kings so seriously that he saw himself as the sole and sacred conduit between God and the Russian people. Even his language changed and he began issuing orders in the manner of a religious prophet. The people must pay for their sins against God and he, the tsar, would be the instrument of his justice. This mania continued as Ivan the Terrible declined further into morbid paranoia. His second and third wives both died in mysterious circumstances convincing him that, like Anastasia, they, too, had been poisoned by unidentified enemies. Then in another bout of manic violence in July 1570 he suddenly ordered the arrest and execution of some of his most loyal servants. Letters to his friend Prince Kurbsky show how he attempted to justify his actions without showing a trace of pity for either his victims or their families. He even claimed that he wanted every relative exterminated so that there would be no one left alive to pray for the souls of the dead.

Ivan's total lack of pity was abnormal even for a tyrant at that time. Behind this pitiless cruelty lurked an obsession with the occult that was almost as powerful as his fascination with Christianity. He believed in the power of black magic and influence of witches and wizards – a fear inherited from his superstitious parents. Even natural phenomena could terrify him – as when on 11 November 1572 a brilliant supernova star appeared in the sky above Moscow. Ivan took this as an omen of disasters to come, such as his loss of the Russian throne.

Isolated in the Kremlin with his terrified court, his only remaining close relationship was with his eldest son and heir, the tsarevitch. Then on 19 November 1581 the violent mania returned.

Ivan suddenly began raging against his son's pregnant wife, screaming and shouting that the clothes she wore were immodest. He then began to beat her violently until she miscarried her baby. When his son burst into the room and began protesting Ivan raised the pointed iron staff he always carried and struck his son a violent blow to the head. Fatally wounded, the young man lay in a coma for several days before dying. Overcome with remorse, Ivan walked behind his son's coffin to the grave repeatedly banging his head against it. Inconsolable, the next day he took a large measure of liquid mercury to dull his grief. Exhumation of his body later showed that he had indeed died of mercury poisoning but also that his bones showed signs of syphilitic ostratis, and mercury was a long-established treatment for this venereal disease. Mercury had been involved in the manic behaviour and eventual death of an earlier tyrant, Emperor Qin of China.

Aside from the effects of mercury addiction it has been suggested that Ivan's unpredictable behaviour was the result of lifelong manic depression. It was certainly one of the key factors in the political pathologies of many tyrants. The tsar's suggested bipolarity could have caused him to switch from depraved orgies to prayers and fasting in a monastery within a short space of time. There is also a suggested link between Napoleon's manic triumphalism in battle and the rapid descent into depression that was reported by his colleagues. Again Hitler's characteristic mood swings are typical of such a personality. When manic, Hitler was egotistical, arrogant, grandiose, loquacious, aggressive, and irritable; he had delusions of omnipotence, invincibility and infallibility. His overwhelming emotional force and persuasiveness, both symptoms of mania, were instrumental in infecting millions of his fellow countrymen with his paranoid delusions. Hitler's 'down' phase was demonstrated when he became depressive: he was despairing, indecisive, isolated and unable to care for himself; he could not concentrate or remember. He washed his hands constantly because of an obsessive fear of germs that may be relevant to his phobic aversion of and paranoid delusions about Jews as contaminants – and the compulsive need to try and cleanse the world of them.

His recorded phobias – including dread of horses, water and the Moon – are as bizarre as Muammar Gaddafi's fear of flying over water and aversion to high buildings, add to this violent mood swings, rages, racing thoughts and pressured speech. To the world he was a ruthless tyrant, wilful, indifferent to the suffering of others, intolerant of criticism and with a consuming need to dominate others. Hitler's one stable element among his violent mood oscillations was hatred. At one time or another he is said to have detested Jews, Jehovah's Witnesses, golfers, Roman Catholics, Poles, Gypsies, gays, communists, skiers, hunters, journalists, judges, smokers, poets, Freemasons and anybody not a vegetarian. He even once revealed that he secretly hated the German middle class.

Could such a man as Adolf Hitler be classified as a sane human being? Certainly he seemed to trust those around him far more than the usual tyrant, often consulting them strategically and in detail – notably in military campaigns. He appeared to have particular faith in Himmler and the SS, although the Reichsführer would betray him in the last days of the war. Some officers, however, doubted Hitler's sanity from the beginning. In 1938 Lieutenant Colonel Hans Oster of German Forces Intelligence involved generals Ludwig Beck, Walther von Brauschitch, Erwin von Witzleben and Franz Halder, together with Admiral Wilhelm Canaris, in a plot to overthrow Hitler: they planned to have him declared insane then to shut him away in a mental hospital. The trigger was to have been Britain's rejection of Germany's Sudetenland demands. However, when the British government capitulated to the Führer they abandoned the plot. This well-documented event suggests that Hitler's sanity was being questioned even at that time. After the war historians began to examine Hitler's sanity in greater detail.

One, Robert Waite, became convinced that Hitler was a psychopath and clinically insane. In fact Hitler acted normally most of the time; although he was clearly a hypochondriac and suffered from a myriad of physical ailments this could not explain his criminal actions. His personal doctor, Dr Theodor Morell, questioned the suggestion of Allied intelligence that the Führer was a serious drug addict although he did prescribe amphetamines for him during the war. This was not uncommon during such a period of great tension. Certainly Hitler never showed symptoms of an addictive personality and neither drank alcohol nor smoked cigarettes. This did nothing to convince the Allies' psychiatrists that Hitler was not insane and that to discover the exact nature of his mental condition might help win the war. The US government agreed, and the Office of Strategic Services was ordered to continue the investigation and to produce a detailed psychological report on Hitler. Particular attention was given to the fact that while his three brothers had died Hitler himself had survived both childhood and the dangers of one of the most dangerous battlefields of the First World War. This appeared to have produced in him the belief that God had spared him to complete a messianic task that would redeem Germany; this might explain why he grew a Christ-like beard when the war ended.

In later years psychiatrists Jerrold Post and Amatzia Baram investigated the mental state of Saddam Hussein. They determined that he was clinically sane but described him as a malignant narcissist – a condition identified as a severe personality disorder. Saddam could be detached, self-centred, oversensitive to criticism and unable to feel empathy for others, while presenting an arrogant façade to the outside world. Malignant narcissists like him are paranoid and aggressive while also lacking moral and ethical judgement. None of this hindered Saddam from being a clever and manipulating tyrant. His self-confidence armed him with a powerful defence mechanism when allied with cruel and sadistic behaviour. Dr Post thought that Saddam's underground bunker, similar to that of Hitler in Berlin, was a physical metaphor for his character. Beneath the grandiose façade of his marble palace lay the inner sanctum, a grim cellar built of steel and reinforced concrete and steel.

12
SEXUAL DEPRAVITY

In Ancient Greece the tyrant stood apart from the rest of humanity, enviable for the power and freedom he enjoyed but terrifying because he was a person who could break all the rules of society, particularly the sexual. The result was rage against good men, whose lives were a reproach to him, and a determination to exploit his power over people in the most outrageous way. There is no better example of this than the mythical figure of Oedipus, the tyrant of Thebes who murdered his father and married his mother. This was an act of incestuous violence that an oracle, early in his life, predicted he would commit. Terrified, he did everything in his power to escape his destiny yet failed; in response, he tore his eyes out, blinding himself to escape the horrid deeds he had carried out. Sigmund Freud appropriated the Greek myth of Oedipus to explore the perverse bond between parents and children of the opposite sex.

Most of these tales of the perversity of tyrants involve aggressive sex, sex under pressure or compulsion. The stories prey on fears of what a tyrant might do given unlimited power. One example is Peisistratos, who seized power in Athens in 546 BC. He placated his opponents by agreeing to marry the daughter of Megakles, one of these opponents. However, he refused to sleep with her except by performing sodomy – so preventing her from having children. When Megakles heard of this he reunited with his political enemies determined to overthrow Peisistratos. This episode confirmed to the Athenians that tyrants practise outlandish and perverted forms of sex. Other stories soon followed. Periander of Corinth was said to have committed incest with his mother, then killed his wife Melissa and committed necrophilia with her corpse. Harder to assess is the outrage perpetrated by Aristodemos of Kymai, who, according to Plutarch, 'outdid himself in baseness by his unjust conduct towards women and free-born boys'. This outrage seems merely to have made the boys grow their hair long and wear jewellery like girls and to have made the girls dress like boys. Whatever Aristodemos' purposes this enforced cross-dressing was a violation of the current sexual norm.

There was also some sympathy for the tyrant for such a man could never know the delights of longing when he could gratify his desire immediately, and he would never know whether his beloved's favours were granted willingly or under compulsion. As Plutarch wrote, 'The tyrant can never be sure that he is loved.' Plutarch described many instances of tyrants who compelled innocent woman to submit to their lust and of the women who preferred to die rather than submit. One such tyrant was Nisaios of Syracuse who was particularly brutal towards women and children. Philip V of Macedonia was a shameless womanizer, and if a woman refused him he would take noisy bands of revellers to her house to annoy her. Those who opposed the tyrant's lust became heroes – such as the lovers Aristogiton and Harmodius whose self-sacrificing courage in slaying the tyrant Hipparchus in the defence of democracy was one of the most important symbolic acts in all Greek history.

Of the Roman tyrants Elagabalus was one of the most notorious – and his name has become synonymous with Roman sexual depravity; he was certainly one of the most intriguing and unusual characters ever to sit on the Roman throne. Just fourteen years old when he became emperor and only eighteen when the Praetorians murdered him and threw his body, along with that of his mother, into the sewers, he was an eccentric hedonist who in his short and tumultuous reign made unprecedented changes to Roman state religion and defied all taboos. He was an oriental boy-priest from Syria who served as the temple of the Roman-

Syrian sun god Elagabal or Elagabalus. He was elevated to power in AD 218. Worship of Elagabalus had always taken place in the sun-god's temple at Emesa (modern Homs in western Syria): when the new emperor arrived in Rome it was made clear to everyone that he intended to continue his duties as a priest of Elagabal. In spite of public outrage, a great temple was built on the Palatine hill, the so-called Elagaballium, the temple of Elagabal, to hold the holy stone. In AD 220 the Senate voted him the title 'Most Magnificent Priest of the Invincible Sun-god Elagabal'. As a priest Elagabalus continued to make sacrifices, laying slaughtered cattle and sheep on the altars and then drenching the carcasses with the finest wines. Afterwards he danced around the altar to the sound of cymbals, flutes and drums, fascinating those who saw him.

His sexual orientation was just as exotic. He married the Vestal Virgin Severa in AD 220 possibly to be seen to conform to Roman custom, but within a year he had divorced her and married Annia Faustina instead. From this he gained much needed credibility, for among her ancestors was Emperor Marcus Aurelius. This did not dispel the criticism of the Roman people, for Annia's husband had been executed on Elagabalus' orders only a short time before. This marriage was just as short-lived, Elagabalus abandoning it and claiming that he had never truly divorced Aquilia Severa in the first place. This was apparently not to be the end of Elagabalus' marital adventures, for according to one account he went on to have no fewer than five wives during his brief reign.

Instead of representing the best of Roman virtues as an emperor notionally should, Elagabalus was seen as an 'Oriental', an alien who wore the garb of a Syrian priest, a long-sleeved tunic that extended down to his feet and was easily confused with female dress. To make matters worse he consistently put make-up on his face. Indeed, the list of un-Roman offences ascribed to the ruler nicknamed 'the Assyrian' is almost endless. His appearance was decidedly un-Roman, too. He wore very costly, silken clothes embroidered with gold because he detested the coarse Greek and Roman garments made of wool, a cheap material in his opinion. While the Romans were used to their emperors, even the mighty Trajan, having a liking for young boys they were shocked by Elagabalus. He was not only an overt transvestite but also an open bisexual.

In spite of his experiments with conventional marriage it became obvious that Elagabalus was basically homosexual, for his interests clearly lay with men, and he seemed to have shown little desire for any of his wives. Apart from his effeminacy, Elagabalus seemed to want to go further and to actually become a woman. He had the hairs plucked from his body and delighted in appearing in public wearing a wig and make-up. Often he dressed as a woman with his eyes painted, his cheeks rouged and his body depilated all over. It was rumoured that he had promised his physicians large sums of money if they could find away to operate on him and actually transform him into a woman. Always highly promiscuous, Elagabalus would sometimes present himself as a prostitute and offer himself naked to passers-by in the grounds of his palace or even in the local taverns. Contemporary Roman historian Cassius Dio wrote that he 'set aside a room in the palace and there committed his indecencies, always standing nude at the door of the room as the harlots do and in a soft and melting voice he solicited the passers by'. Elagabalus also created a public bath inside the palace, so that he could collect paramours with remarkable phallic endowments. He took to frequenting the notorious brothels, driving out to the prostitutes and playing the role himself. Frustrated at being unable to change sex completely, he considered castrating himself but settled for being circumcised instead. There were other, darker sexual imperatives, too. Cassius Dio claimed that Elagabalus was often thrashed by his lovers and bore the marks of the beating all over his body. Even more infuriating to the people of Rome than his sexual antics was the appointment of some of his low-born lovers to the highest offices of state.

Elagabalus had become an unbearable emperor for the Roman people. The plotting began, led by his maternal grandmother Julia Maesa, who decided that the young emperor and his mother Julia Soaemias, who increasingly encouraged his religious fervour, must go. She turned to her younger daughter Julia Avita Mamaea, who had a thirteen-year-old son, Alexianus, and the two women managed to persuade Elagabalus to adopt Alexianus as his heir. They explained to him that this would allow him more time to spend on his religious duties, as Alexianus would take over his ceremonial obligations. Soon afterwards, in late AD 221, Elagabalus changed his mind and attempted to have Alexander assassinated. Perhaps by then he had realized what his grandmother intended. The plotters were forced to act and they bribed the Praetorian Guard to kill Elagabalus when he visited their camp on 11 March 222. He was set upon by the troops and beheaded; his body was dragged through the streets of Rome and thrown into the River Tiber. Ever since his assassination by the Praetorian Guard at the age of eighteen, Elagabalus has been an object of fascination to historians and a source of inspiration for artists and writers.

A reliable account of the almost surreal depravity of another Roman tyrant, Tiberius, is given by the author Suetonius. On retiring to Capri Tiberius indulged in secret orgies that involved teams of sexual athletes of both sexes who were experts in deviant intercourse and dubbed *analists*; they copulated before him in triple unions to excite his flagging passions. The bedrooms of the imperial villa were decorated with salacious paintings and sculptures and equipped with an erotic library, in case a performer should need an illustration of what was required. In the surrounding woods the emperor arranged a series of woody groves in which boys and girls dressed as the god Pan or as nymphs solicited outside bowers and grottoes. The people openly called Tiberius' pleasure ground 'the old goat's garden' – a pun on the island's name. His grosser depravities became the subject of legend – for example, he reputedly trained little boys, known as his 'tiddlers', to crawl between his thighs when he went swimming and nibble at his genitals; unweaned babies were said to be used for the same purpose. On the wall of his bedroom hung a painting entitled *Atalanta Pleasuring Meleager with Her Lips*. The story is also told that once at a sacrifice, attracted by the acolyte's beauty, he lost control of himself and, hardly waiting for the ceremony to end, rushed him off and debauched him and the acolyte's brother, the flute-player, too. Subsequently, when they complained of the assault, he had their legs broken. His habit of abusing women even of high birth is shown by the death of a certain Mallonia who had been brought to his bed but vigorously refused to submit to his lust. She was put on trial and verbally abused so badly that she eventually committed suicide. The people had revenge of sorts a short while later when one of the new plays at the theatre satirized the 'old goat'.

After the death of Tiberius Suetonius also provided a salacious account of his successor, Caligula. The new emperor, he commented, showed little sexual restraint with either men or women and was said to have engaged in homosexual relationships, 'both active and passive, with Marcus Lepidus, Mnester the comedian and various foreign hostages'. Another of his contemporaries, Valerius Catullus, a young man of a consular family, even boasted publicly that he had buggered the emperor and quite worn himself out in the process. Caligula seemed proud of his amorality claiming that he had not the slightest regard for chastity, either his own or that of others. As well these homosexual encounters he made advances to almost every woman of rank in Rome. In addition to incest with his sisters he displayed a wild passion for the prostitute Pyrallis. After inviting a selection of noble women to dinner he would slowly and carefully examine each in turn as they passed his couch, as a purchaser might assess the value of a slave, and even stretch out his hand and lift up the chin of any woman who kept her eyes modestly cast down. Then whenever he felt so inclined he would send for whoever pleased him best and leave the banquet in her company. A little later he would return, showing obvious signs of what he had been about, and openly discuss his bedfellow in detail, dwelling on her good and bad physical points and commenting on her sexual performance. To some of these unfortunates he issued, and publicly registered, divorces in the names of their absent husbands.

Suetonius also left a scurrilous account of the sexual debauchery of a third Roman emperor, Nero. He was convinced that the cause of Nero's transformation from virtue to depravity, violence and unmitigated squander was sexual. The young, handsome Nero had been obsessed with music, the theatre and art and with giving public recitals of his poems, but as he aged he began to throw wild dinner parties to which he invited prostitutes; Suetonius gives an alarming account of the rapacity and the extremes of sexuality that took place. Although Nero's first experiments with debauchery were relatively mild his sexual appetites soon drove him through the catalogue of lusts – and his appetite for carnal pleasure increased dramatically, leading to ever-greater perversions as he continued to experiment. Soon he appeared to be almost out of control as Suetonius laments:

> Not satisfied with seducing free-born boys and married women, Nero raped the Vestal Virgin Rubria . . . Having tried to turn the boy Sporus into a girl by castration, he went through a wedding ceremony with him – dowry, bridal veil and all – which the whole court attended, then . . . treated him as a wife. He dressed Sporus in the fine clothes normally worn by an empress and took him in his own litter not only to every Greek assize and fair but actually through the Street of Images at Rome, fondly kissing him from time to time . . . A rather amusing joke is still going the rounds: the world would have been a happier place had Nero's father Domitius married that sort of wife . . . His feasts now lasted from noon till

midnight, with occasional break for diving into a warm bath or, if it were summer, into snow-cooled water. Sometimes he would hold public dinner parties in the Campus Martius, with prostitutes and dancing girls from all over the city among his guests.

Nero's flagrant disregard for traditional Roman morality reached its peak in his behaviour towards his own family. He conceived an unnatural attachment to his own mother in the manner of Oedipus that shocked patrician society. Even in Nero's day the crossing of this sexual line had terrible repercussions. Here again Suetonius worked his favourite theme: the sexual instinct, because it constantly seeks new forms of arousal, proceeds to the corruption of all moral norms. Nero's later murder of his mother, Agrippina, is often represented as the most startling example of incestuous sadism. Nero attempted the murder at least four times before he succeeded at last, making Agrippina one of the most persecuted mothers in Western history. Although Nero's motives for the crime were mixed, Suetonius shows that there was a strong sexual undercurrent of sadism in Nero's character as he also murdered his favourite aunt by ordering her doctors to give her a laxative of fatal strength. Moreover he treated his first wife appallingly by attempting to strangle her on a number of occasions, and although he doted on his second wife he kicked her to death while she was pregnant because she dared complain that he came home late from the races.

Compared to the excesses of Ancient Greece and Rome later tyrants seems almost conventional in their sexual debauchery – using their powers to indulge in heterosexual affairs. The exception, of course, is Ivan the Terrible, who seemed obsessed with exploring the whole catalogue of sexual perversions. In the twentieth century Benito Mussolini made a memorable contribution, once telling his jealous lover Clara Petacci that the idea of sleeping with just one woman was inconceivable to him and that there had been a period in his life when 'I had fourteen women, and I'd take three or four every evening, one after the other . . . that gives you an idea of my sexuality.' According to Petacci's diaries, Mussolini's trysts occurred anywhere the fancy took him, on the carpet or against a wall, and ended abruptly, without 'coffee, liqueur, or even a piece of cake' as she put it. Describing the first night they spent together in his villa in Rome she recalls that 'After the first assault, in which he achieved complete satisfaction, we started all over again . . . He never even appeared slightly tired . . . I'd never seen such passion for sex with a woman . . . I was honest when he asked me if I'd enjoyed myself. It didn't seem right to lie. He obviously took this as a challenge and began again.' Clara went on to describe another typical encounter, 'I hold him tightly. I kiss him and we make love with such fury that his screams seem like those of a wounded beast'; she also recalled, 'We made love with such force that he bit my shoulder so hard his teeth left a mark.' Mussolini himself admitted that he regarded all women as prostitutes: sex with them, he said, was 'like screwing a whore'; they existed simply for his 'carnal pleasure'. Today his violent behaviour seems almost criminal and deeply disturbing, particularly his claim that women prefer men to be brutal 'like cavalry soldiers'. He thought they should tremble at the power of his love-making, comparing it to a 'cyclone, uprooting everything in its path'. He claimed to have told one lover he that wished he could have 'entered [her] on a horse'. He certainly suffered from considerable *post coitum triste* (post-coital sadness) in the aftermath of such encounters, often feeling disgusted, not of course at his own behaviour but at the women who had submitted to it. 'I am an animal,' he liked to brag but 'afterwards I felt nothing but disgust. I wanted to beat her up, throw her on the floor.' One historian has calculated that Mussolini enjoyed the favours of at least five thousand women during his lifetime. Towards the end of his twenty-three-year dictatorship, however, as Italy faced defeat he became addicted to a German-manufactured aphrodisiac pill trademarked Hormovin. He saw taking this prototype Viagra as a 'political act' because it served to prolong the myth of Il Duce as one who never flagged. Throughout his dictatorship sex was at the centre of the myth of Mussolini; it was indeed at the centre of his life but without any accompaniment of love or romance. Fascism, as its anthem 'Giovinezza' proclaimed, exalted youth and with it both virility and violence. Mussolini's carefully nurtured masculine image helped him to power, just as power enabled him to have as varied a sex life as he wanted. That potency then encouraged him to delusions of invincibility, to squander both his country's credit and resources on wars that he regarded as virility contests.

More recent tyrants have been careful to behave with more discretion but even essentially mundane dictators such as the Ceauşescus of Romania have revealed a controversial sex life. Elena Ceauşescu worked in a bar-cum-brothel when she first arrived in Bucharest from the countryside as a teenager. Nicolae Ceauşescu's brother, Nicolae-Andruta, testified that one day in 1943 he found his wife and Elena naked with two German officers when Nicolae Ceauşescu was in prison at the time. Once they were in power, palace spies say she always initiated sex. Nicolae was not above instructing his spies to use sexual entrapment; Nicolae and Elena watched blue movies together – special ones made by the Romanian intelligence service showing Western diplomats in compromising positions. Elena was also obsessed with the sexual peccadilloes of the Politburo wives. She had the Romanian intelligence service bug them so she could listen to the sounds they made when they made love.

It is difficult to associate Joseph Stalin with sexual deviancy, because he appeared too guarded to have ever risked such an encounter. However, there were rumours in his lifetime that when in his thirties he had raped or seduced, even fathered a child with a girl who was just thirteen years old and had been indicted for the under-age seduction by the police. On his death in 1953 the rumours resurfaced, and Nikita Khrushchev commissioned his KGB boss General Ivan Serov to investigate in great secrecy. Serov reported back to Khrushchev that amazingly the entire story of Stalin's affair with a thirteen-year-old was true. Khrushchev showed it to the Politburo, including Stalin's long-serving henchman Molotov, who all signed it and then filed it in the deepest recesses of the archives where it has remained until now.

But Stalin's depravity cannot be compared to that of Lavrenty Beria, the head of the secret police, the NKVD. Beria was responsible for overseeing the murder of millions of Russians, some shot at night in the depths of the Lubyanka, the secret police headquarters, others dragged off to the gulags. For decades after he was shot any mention of Beria was expunged from official Soviet records. Unlike Stalin, who was buried in Lenin's Mausoleum and later moved to a grave by the Kremlin walls, Beria's body was burned and his ashes dispersed by a huge fan. Charges of sexual assault and deviance against him were first made in a speech by a secretary of the central committee of the Communist Party, Nikolay Shatalin, in July 1953, two weeks after Beria's arrest. Shatalin said that Beria had had sexual relations with numerous women and that he had contracted syphilis as a result of his sex with prostitutes. Shatalin referred to a list, supposedly kept by Beria's bodyguard, of more than twenty-five women with whom Beria had sex. Over time, however, the charges became more dramatic. Khrushchev wrote in his posthumously published memoirs, 'We were given a list of more than a hundred names of women. They were dragged to Beria by his people. And he had the same trick for them all: all who got to his house for the first time, Beria would invite for a dinner and would propose to drink for the health of Stalin. And in wine he would mix in some sleeping pills.' More evidence appeared of his deep depravity as a sexual predator.

At night Beria would cruise the streets of Moscow seeking out teenage girls. When he saw one who took his fancy he would have his guards deliver her to his house. One witness, Anton Antonov-Ovseyenko, said, 'Sometimes he would have his henchmen bring five, six or seven girls to him. He would make them strip, except for their shoes, and then force them into a circle on their hands and knees with their heads together. He would walk around in his dressing-gown inspecting them. Then he would pull one out by her leg and haul her off to rape her. He called it the flower game.' Even fellow senior communists, many of them mass murderers in their own right, had nothing good to say about Beria, describing him as slippery and obsequious in front of his superiors but brutal and cunning behind their backs. One account says Beria personally strangled his predecessor, Nikolai Yezhov.

Of all the tyrants of the twentieth century, Hitler has exerted the most fascination in terms of his sex life, leading to thousands of pages of discussion and speculation. Entire books have been devoted to the subject and the Führer diagnosed as Hitler the copromaniac, Hitler the homosexual and Hitler the heterosexual. All these suggestions have their origin in the testimony of individuals who became critics of Hitler. For instance, the claim that Hitler defecated on his niece Geli Raubal came from Otto Strasser, a dissenting Nazis who was driven out of the country. The claim that Hitler had had a homosexual affair in the trenches came from Hans Mend, a comrade from the First World War who later died in a Nazi prison. What is clear is that Hitler was such a monster that the public were quite prepared to believe him capable of the most disgusting sexual aberrations.

The best known of his heterosexual relationships was with Eva Braun who was his lover from 1932 onwards. They generally slept apart, and Hitler's butler remarked after the war that he had never seen any evidence of sexual relations between the two, despite careful examination. Although physically unappealing Hitler proved surprisingly attractive and in some cases totally magnetic to women – such as the English fascist Unity Mitford. Historians know of perhaps eight lovers in all, but half of them are doubtful prospects. There are also reports of Hitler finding it difficult to kiss or make love. Mimi Reiter, a young girlfriend, described how he clenched his fists whenever he tried to kiss her, 'He didn't know what to do,' she said. Later in their relationship, though, everything seems to have gone much more smoothly, at least on the sexual plane. Other aspects of the affair must have been less happy for after a particularly fraught encounter she tried to hang herself. Uncannily, of the eight women mentioned as possible lovers, four tried to commit suicide or succeeded in killing themselves and even Eva Braun made two suicide attempts while she was with him. Others have concluded that Hitler was a member of a minority group that according to sexual researcher Alfred Kinsey composes just 1.5 per cent of the male population – the asexual. Clearly he was not driven by a powerful libido although he did have an aesthetic sense that this or that woman was attractive to him. He certainly wanted to be adored, but he did not seem to be particularly concerned about sex with anyone or anything: man, woman or animal.

Then there is the question of Hitler's genitals. The Nazi leader was said to have lost a testicle during the Battle of the Somme in 1916. The medical condition, for which there has never been conclusive proof, was mocked in the Second World War ditty which begins: 'Hitler has only got one ball.' The truth is that no one who survived the war could say for certain what Hitler's genitals looked like. The dictator was pathologically reluctant to let even his own personal doctors examine him intimately – in fact this reluctance is the main reason many people suspect he must have had some sort of deformity. According to the historian David Irving Hitler's principal doctor, Theo Morrell, conducted many examinations of the Nazi leader's upper body but was never allowed to go 'further south'. Other historians claim that a detailed examination of his speeches revealed the frequent use of words such as 'dirt', 'filth', 'dung' and 'smell', which could be ascribed to poor toilet training and motherly neglect at an important period of his childhood. Similarly, it has been suggested that Hitler might have developed an Oedipus complex about his mother and feared symbolic castration by his father as a punishment. This led in turn to a fear of syphilis and an aversion to physical contact; those who support this theory intimate that his relationship with Eva Braun was unconsummated. Some people have also suggested that Hitler enjoyed looking at other men's bodies and had strong, if sublimated, homosexual tendencies.

13
DECEPTIVE NORMALITY

While the great majority of tyrants have displayed unpredictable and eccentric behaviour there are some who have attempted to present themselves as moderate and reasonable. Whatever the hidden brutality of their regime, as leaders they presented themselves as sober and respectable politicians. Such a man was Dr António Salazar, who became dictator of Portugal in 1932 and set out to maintain an image of middle-class normality in both his behaviour and appearance. This may well have been provoked by witnessing the excesses of the personality cults that had arisen in the early twentieth century in Italy, Russia and Germany. In the sixteen years before he came to power there had been twenty-four revolutions in Portugal and no fewer than 158 general strikes and forty-four changes of government. Whatever else he brought Salazar certainly introduced political stability to his country. He maintained his low-profile rule until 1974. A sombre figure, he never encouraged the mass rallies and military displays characteristic of the Mussolini regime in Italy or that of General Franco in Spain. Instead he was always a low-key presence appropriate to the image of a man who was resolved to promote the traditional Roman Catholic morality of Portugal. This did not, however, stop him from keeping an iron grip on Portuguese society. Coincidentally he had, like Joseph Stalin, once considered becoming a priest before studying law at Coimbra University in 1914. Here his reserved manner and refusal to shake hands with his students after a lecture earned him the sobriquet 'the man of ice'. Both his reserved manner and his conservative political ideas derived from a passionate commitment to Roman Catholicism. So strong was his faith that he took to the streets with others to oppose the socialism of the Portuguese First Republic.

In character Salazar was a painfully shy and highly reserved man who abhorred public ceremonies and would have preferred living in isolation if his civic duties had not made this impossible. A conformist even in his extremism Salazar introduced a new constitution that owed much to the new fascist systems that already existed in Germany and Italy. For his first cabinet he chose technocrats rather than professional politicians, among them an engineer, a lawyer and a soldier. These men helped him to balance the Portuguese budget for the first time but at the price of national austerity. Yet perhaps uniquely as a dictator Salazar was quite prepared to share the hardship with his people. Unmarried, he lived in a small apartment of just three rooms, eating frugally, buying his own coal and paying his servants out of his modest prime ministerial salary of just $125 a week. He neither smoked, drank alcohol nor held parties. His motivation was from a sense of duty rather than generosity, preferring to be respected rather than loved. When a grateful peasant once presented him with a gift as he opened a bridge Salazar gently rebuked him saying, 'You don't have to thank me. I do everything to help you but nothing to please you!'

With the essential support of both the army and the security police, Salazar imposed an authoritarian rule on Portugal. Neither as bloody as other the dictatorships nor as obsessed with the glorification of the leader or the party, Salazar's Portugal was nevertheless a modern police state. Unlike Fascist Italy the new Portugal did not pursue a policy of latter-day colonial expansion, but it quietly maintained its established and sizeable empire in Africa. Domestically Salazar pursued a conservative social policy that he called the *Estado Novo* or 'new state'. Under this Portugal remained stable while enjoying only a modest amount of economic growth. Although corporate in nature it revealed a strong Roman Catholic and anti-materialistic influence, being clearly based on the conservative papal encyclicals *Rerum Novarum* and *Quad-ragesimo Anno*.

Under Salazar, Portugal was run for thirty-five years as a quiet, bourgeois dictatorship with a sober-living leader and the Roman Catholic Church as the arbiter of its ethical system. The main enemy of right-wing dictatorships at the time was, of course, international communism, the principal export of Soviet Russia. To control the state and oppose the left-wing organizations that predictably rose up, Salazar placed his trust in the PIDE or secret police. This was an organization that he created with the German Gestapo as his model. The PIDE went about its unpleasant work with a minimum of violence, although Portuguese dissidents were vigorously, if less brutally, pursued. By comparison with other totalitarian tyrannies Salazar's regime was moderate, although independent historians claim that sixty political prisoners died in Portuguese gaols during Salazar's rule of nearly forty years.

Aware of Karl Popper's dictum that a society can be threatened from the right as well as from the left Salazar was careful not to allow more extreme right-wing influences to gain control. Eventually he banned the National Syndicalists, Portugal's main fascist party, altogether for being 'too pagan and too totalitarian'. As befitted the little world to which Portugal had been reduced his own party, the National Union, existed merely to support the regime and promoted little else, ignoring the outside world and its dangerous political theories. Although careful to keep his distance politically there is no doubt that Salazar maintained great sympathy for Fascist Italy and admired what Mussolini was doing there. He was equally sympathetic to General Franco and gave him his full support during the Spanish Civil War. In many ways Franco and Salazar complemented each other – even to the extent of keeping their countries neutral in the Second World War, in spite of the obvious temptation to join in on Hitler's side in the early years. Unlike the German and Italian regimes Portugal under Salazar shied away from any spectacular economic reforms.

There was no mobilization of labour, no vast infrastructure projects like the autobahns. As a result of Salazar's highly conservative economic policies the wealth of the ruling oligarchy increased significantly while the Portuguese people became among the poorest in Europe. The much-vaunted stability that he had delivered led only to stagnation in the long term and was compounded by Salazar's own distrust of materialism. As the years passed he remained convinced that any significant rise in Portuguese living standards would inevitably 'leave in darkness all that is spiritual in the human being'. In other words it was important to keep the people poor in order to maintain the pious Roman Catholic ethics of the state. Inevitably this led to his being wary of providing an open educational system that might allow the Portuguese people to develop dangerous and subversive ideas. For this reason spending on higher education was carefully controlled and all literature and publications were heavily censored as a precaution. Obedience and acceptance of one's lot were the order of the day. Suspicious by nature, Salazar made the administration of Portugal peculiarly his own, delegating little and taking a hands-on approach to every aspect of government. The result was a form of national apathy; the people gave up even attempting to have a say in the running of their country.

The nation's isolationism was compounded by another of Salazar's eccentricities, his reluctance to travel abroad after the Second World War. He became a kind of King Canute of foreign affairs at a time when other European countries were giving up their colonial possessions. As the tide of nationalism swept Africa and the Far East, Salazar stubbornly refused to even contemplate allowing Portugal's overseas possessions to gain their independence. This provoked the United Nations to demand to know why Portuguese colonies used forced labour at just twelve cents a day, provided no education for natives and flogged and tortured them for minor offences. Small wonder that his colourless obscurantism appeared increasingly irrelevant in the late twentieth century. As a result of Salazar's inward-looking policies Portugal became a latter-day version of José Gaspar Francia's Paraguay a century earlier, an isolated country largely cut off from the rest of a world when momentous events were taking place. Salazar's obsession with keeping out of the limelight meant that there was little evidence of national or international ambition. His sole concern appeared to be the prolongation of the status quo and what passed for normality.

One contemporary tyrant who has shown a deceptive image of normality is President Bashar al-Assad of Syria. Never one to embrace gaudy military uniforms or display an aggressive, over-confident manner, Assad appeared the epitome of moderation until the recent civil war began. Mundane in appearance, he dressed as soberly as António Salazar ever did. Differing from the public perception of a tyrant, Assad appeared to be a good family man and was often photographed with his attractive wife and children. His early life was almost conventional for a man who was the son of Hafez al-Assad, the ruthless tyrant of Syria, and he was well educated with a declared sympathy for humanist ideas. His chosen career was a surprise: a doctor specializing in ophthalmology, first in Damascus and then at the Western Eye Hospital in London. So far, so conventional. As a medical student in London Bashar was reported as being shy, retiring and keen to succeed in his profession. Socially he kept a low profile, living modestly if comfortably; by all accounts he was a quiet, polite and careful doctor who was always pleasant to his patients and respectful of his seniors.

'Papa Doc' Duvalier of Haiti once said that a nation's ills demand a doctor, and it is curious how many tyrants and terrorists studied medicine when young. William Walker, the homicidal president and generalissimo of Nicaragua in 1856, was a doctor – as was Dr Félix Houphouët-Boigny, the Francophile despot of the Ivory Coast who was fascinated by grandiose schemes. He decided to build a vast cathedral in the middle of the jungle, even larger than St Peter's in Rome. Another doctor/dictator was Dr

Hastings Banda of Malawi, whose medical training did not stop him from imposing a forty-year reign of terror on his country; before coming to power he had practised in the USA and Britain and specialized in venereal diseases. Radovan Karadži , the Bosnian Serb leader, was also a doctor; his medical experience did not dissuade him from actions that led to his being put on trial for crimes against humanity. Moreover some of the most ruthless terrorist leaders have trained as doctors, including Dr Ayman al-Zawahiri, Osama bin Laden's lieutenant who masterminded the 9/11 atrocity. Again the ex-leader of the PFLP Palestinians in the 1970s, Dr George Habash, and Dr Abdel Rantisi, the Hamas leader behind the suicide bombings of the 1990s, were both trained and practising doctors. There is a simple explanation for this, for at that time in the developing world most talented and well-educated young men saw medicine as the only available path out of poverty and into middle-class status.

That Bashar al-Assad could devote himself to medicine was because he was never intended to succeed his father Hafez as the ruler of Syria. That role was reserved for his elder brother Basil. Macho and aggressive, Basil was the favourite son who bullied Bashar while being groomed by his father as the future sole dictator of Syria. Apart from Basil there were other children in the family with psychological qualities much better suited to rule Syria. Everything changed when in 1994 Basil was killed in a car accident caused by his typically wild driving; his father called on Bashar to take on his late brother's role. He was told that that it was his duty was to serve the interests of the family, the party and the state, in that order. If Bashar had been a strong and brave man, he would have refused the poisoned chalice; but, having accepted it, he had to drain it thoroughly. For Bashar al-Assad, it was power or total extinction, not only for himself but for his entire group. Always the pragmatist, Bashar accepted his fate without protest and began preparing himself for the task by taking a crash-course in the workings of the military and government.

At first he appeared to be a refreshing change from the past and a leader of whom great things were expected. 'Syria under the leadership of President Al-Assad will become a model in the Arab world after accomplishing the reforms announced by the Syrian leadership,' the Turkish foreign minister Ahmet Davutoglu was happy to announce. His personal image appeared to support this reading of his character. In private life he seemed to maintain the same normality that he had enjoyed in London. In contrast to his reclusive father, who had rarely been seen at other than formal state occasions, Bashar took his family out to restaurants in Damascus, attended concerts and appeared to emulate the lifestyle of a Western leader. Assad lived in a relatively small house in a normal – albeit guarded – street and believed that his modest lifestyle was an element in his appeal and made him better esteemed by his own people than many other Arab rulers. His wife, the beautiful, educated, anglicized daughter of a successful Syrian physician exiled in London, was no more destined by nature for the role of dictator's wife than he for that of dictator. Her metamorphosis from Mrs Assad to the Eva Peron and then to the Elena Ceauşescu of Syria was caused by events rather by choice.

Bashar began his rule by attempting to modernize the political system that he had inherited. This was abandoned when he began to encounter opposition from the many political factions in Syria. He swiftly decided that this hostility posed a deadly threat to all that he held dear, including the interests of the Alawite clan and the Ba'ath Party. As his actions became ever more tyrannical he attempted to preserve his personal air of normality. A study of him in *Psychology Today* shows how often he uses the language of medical healing and cleansing in his political discourse and regularly talks of the bacterium of Muslim fundamentalism. It also suggests an inner conflict revealed in the frequency with which he uses negative forms in English speech. There may be several of them in one phrase. This indicates that he has a deep feeling of unease in any given conversation but he is sure of doing the right thing and sees no need to change his behaviour. This suggestion of possible reasonableness and moderation disguised an indifference to criticism from those who are outside his family, be it the West, the United Nations, foreign journalists, other Arab countries or protesters in his own country. Their criticism does not touch him because he correlates his self-esteem only with the requirements that tie him up with the father who is Bashar's role model. For years, many Western analysts and diplomats have viewed Assad as malleable, even naïve. His former aides describe a man who is accustomed to being underestimated and adept at exploiting those misperceptions. Before negotiations Assad would tell his team to let the other side think they had won, 'Give them always nice words, nice meetings, nice phrases and they will be happy, they will say good things about us, and they cannot withdraw from it later.'

Throughout his rule and particularly during the civil war there has been a strange mismatch between the normality of his low-key demeanour and the bloody events that have raged throughout Syria. What outsiders have been slow to realize is that in the game Assad is playing, a weak man or one perceived that way can cling to power just as tenaciously, and violently, as a strong man. Over the course of his reign he has learned how to turn his biggest shortcomings – his desire for approval, his tendency toward prevarication – into his greatest assets. He has also shown an almost dispassionate aloofness when addressing the outside world. This may be the result of his growing up in a powerful ruler's court, much as Caligula did under Tiberius, where it was essential not to draw attention to oneself. Another explanation is that he is no longer running the show and the civil war has become so important to his international backers that he has become their virtual puppet. With his receding chin and strange ears Assad gives the appearance of a weak and ordinary man whom you would expect to be more a petty bureaucrat than a brutal tyrant. But push such a man to the wall and he is capable of the greatest obduracy, which is the strength of the weak. A cornered rat, which normally resides incognito, is a ferocious and dangerous beast, even if it remains in essence weak and highly vulnerable.

It seems that most tyrants end their lives as cornered rats – whether it be Emperor Nero shaking with fear as the sound of the approaching soldier's feet echo down the palace corridor or Muammar Gaddafi dragged like a rodent from his hiding place in a sewer in the desert. The lucky ones, of course, escape and end their days in some luxury as the discreet guest of another authoritarian state. None, it seems, take refuge in a democracy these days – since in recent years the International Criminal Court at the Hague might well await them. Increasingly, in the words of the old adage, you can run but you can no longer hide.

FURTHER READING

Abzug, Robert H., *Inside the Vicious Heart: Americans and the Liberation of Nazi Concentration Camps*, Oxford: Oxford University Press, 1985

Adorno, Theodor, Else Frenkel-Brunswik and Daniel Levinson, *The Authoritarian Personality*, New York: W.W. Norton, 1993

al-Khalil, Samir, *Republic of Fear: The Politics of Modern Iraq*, Los Angeles: University of California Press, 1989

Arendt, Hannah, *The Origins of Totalitarianism*, London: André Deutsch, 1986

Aristotle's Politics, translated by Benjamin Jowett, Oxford: Clarendon Press, 1945

Axelrod, Alan, and Charles Phillips, *Dictators and Tyrants: Absolute Rulers and Would-Be Rulers in World History*, New York: Facts on File, 1995

Ayling, S.E., *Portraits of Power: An Introduction to Twentieth-Century History Through the Lives of Seventeen Great Political Leaders*, New York: Barnes and Noble, 1963

Behr, Edward, *Kiss the Hand You Cannot Bite: The Rise and Fall of the Ceauşescus*, London: Penguin Books, 1992

Bosworth, R.J.B., *Mussolini's Italy: Life Under the Fascist Dictatorship, 1915-1945*, London: Penguin Books, 2005

Bouc, Alain, *Mao Tse-tung, A Guide to His Thought*, translated by Paul Auster and Lydia Davis, New York: St Martin's Press, 1977

Bullock, Alan, *Hitler and Stalin: Parallel Lives*, London: HarperCollins, 1991

Chan, Stephen, *Robert Mugabe: A Life of Power and Violence*, London: I.B. Tauris, 2003

Chirot, Daniel, *Modern Tyrants: The Power and Prevalence of Evil in Our Age*, Princeton: Princeton University Press, 1996

Clements, Jonathan, *The First Emperor of China*, Gloucestershire: Sutton Publishing, 2007

Collier, Richard, *Duce!: A Biography of Benito Mussolini*, London: Fontana, 1972

Conquest, Robert, *The Great Terror: Stalin's Purge of the Thirties*, London, Macmillan, 1968

Cousins, Norman, *The Pathology of Power*, New York: W.W. Norton, 1987

Crankshaw, Edward, *Gestapo, Instrument of Tyranny*, New York: Viking Press, 1956

Crassweller, Robert D., *Trujillo: The Life and Times of a Caribbean Dictator*, London: Macmillan, 1966

Crowcroft, Andrew, *The Psychotic: Understanding Madness*, London: Penguin Books, 1975

Davidson, Eugene, *The Making of Adolf Hitler*, New York: Macmillan, 1977

Davies, James C., *Human Nature in Politics: The Dynamics of Political Behavior*, New York: John Wiley and Sons, 1963

Davies, Norman, *Heart of Europe: A Short History of Poland*, Oxford: Oxford University Press, 1986

Decalo, Samuel, *Coups and Army Rule in Africa: Motivation and Constraints*, New Haven: Yale University Press, 1990

Deutscher, Isaac, *Stalin: A Political Biography*, Oxford: Oxford University Press, 1949

Dickie, John, *Cosa Nostra: A History of the Sicilian Mafia*, London, Hodder, 2007

Diederich, Bernard, and Al Burt, *Papa Doc: The Truth About Haiti Today*, London: Penguin Books, 1972

Dirlik, Arif, *The Origins of Chinese Communism*, Oxford: Oxford University Press, 1989

Djilas, Milovan, *Conversations with Stalin*, New York: Harcourt, Brace and World, 1962

Dunlop, Ian, *Louis XIV*, London: Sinclair-Stevenson, 1999

Dwyer, Philip, *Napoleon: The Path to Power 1769–1799*, London: Bloomsbury, 2007

Eagan, James, *Maximilien Robespierre: Nationalist Dictator*, London: Octagon Books, 1978

Elvin, Mark, *The Pattern of the Chinese Past*, Stanford: Stanford University Press, 1973

Englund, Steven, *Napoleon: A Political Life*, Cambridge, Massachusetts:
Harvard University Press, 2005

Everitt, Anthony, *The First Emperor: Caesar Augustus and the Triumph of Rome*,
London: John Murray, 2007

Falasca-Zamponi, Simonetta, *Fascist Spectacle*, Berkeley: University of
California Press, 2000

Ferguson, James, *Papa Doc, Baby Doc: Haiti and the Duvaliers*, Oxford:
Blackwood Publishers, 1988

Fischer, Louis, *The Life of Lenin*, New York: Harper and Row, 1964

Fitzgerald, C.P., *Mao Tse-tung and China*, London: Penguin Books, 1977

Fitzpatrick, Sheila, *The Russian Revolution*, Oxford: Oxford University Press,
1982

Foley, Martin, *Trujillo: Death at a Distance*, Alexandria, Virginia: Washington
House, 2005

Friedlander, Saul, *Nazi Germany and the Jews: Years of Persecution, 1933–39*,
London: Phoenix, 1998

Fromm, Eric, *The Anatomy of Human Destructiveness*, London: Jonathan
Cape, 1974

Fukuyama, Francis, *The End of History and the Last Man*, New York: Free
Press, 1992

Garnier, Christine, *Salazar in Portugal: An Intimate Portrait*, New York:
Farrar, Straus and Young, 1954

Glass, James, *Psychosis and Power: Threats to Democracy in the Self and in the
Group*, Ithaca, NY: Cornell University Press, 1986

Goldberg, Carl, *Speaking with the Devil: A Dialogue with Evil*, New York:
Viking, 1996

Goodwin, Frederick K., and Kay Jamison, *Manic Depressive Illness*, Oxford:
Oxford University Press, 1990

Gwyn, David, *Idi Amin – Death-Light of Africa*, New York: Little, Brown and
Co., 1977

Heitland, W.E., *A Short History of the Roman Republic*, Cambridge:
Cambridge University Press, 1911

Hibbert, Christopher, *Benito Mussolini: The Rise and Fall of Il Duce*, London,
Penguin Books, 1965

Hobsbawm, Eric, *The Age of Capital 1848–1875*, New York: Charles Scribner's, 1975

Hoxha, Enver, *The Artful Albanian: The Memoirs of Enver Hoxha*, edited and introduced by Jon Halliday, London: Chatto and Windus, 1986

Hyde, H. Montgomery, *Stalin: The History of a Dictator*, London: Hart-Davis, 1971

Ionescu, Ghita, *Communism in Romania 1944–1962*, Oxford: Oxford University Press, 1964

James, C.L.R, *The Black Jacobins: Toussaint L'Ouverture and the San Domingo Revolution*, New York: Vintage, 1963

Johnson, A. H., *The Age of the Enlightened Despot 1660–1789*, London: Methuen, 1936

Kaggwa, Apolo, *The Kings of Buganda*, Nairobi: East African Publishing House, 1971

Karsh, Efraim and Inari Rautsi, *Saddam Hussein: A Political Biography*, New York: Free Press, 1991

Kater, Michael H., *The Nazi Party: A Social Profile of Members and Leaders 1919–1956*, Cambridge: Cambridge University Press, 1983

Kay, Hugh, *Salazar and Modern Portugal*, London: Eyre and Spottiswoode, 1970

Kennedy, Paul M., *The Rise of Anglo-German Antagonism 1860–1914*, London: Allen and Unwin, 1980.

Kershaw, Ian, *Hitler*, London: Longman, 1991

Kiernan, Ben, *How Pol Pot Came to Power*, London: Verso, 1985

Klonsky, Milton, *The Fabulous Ego: Absolute Power in History*, New York: Quadrangle/New York Times Book Co., 1974

Kubizek, August, *The Young Hitler I Knew*, translated by E.V. Anderson, London: Greenhill Books, 2006

Kuper, Leo, *Genocide: Its Political Use in the Twentieth Century*, London: Penguin Books, 1981

Laqueur, Walter, *Fascism: Past, Present, Future*, Oxford: Oxford University Press, 1996

Le Bon, Gustave, *The Crowd: A Study of the Popular Mind*, London: Fisher Unwin, 1909

Lee, Stephen, *European Dictatorships 1918–1945*, London: Routledge, 2000

Levy, Arthur, *The Private Life of Napoleon*, translated by Stephen Louis Simeon, London: Richard Bentley and Son, 1894

Lewis, Paul, *Authoritarian Regimes in Latin America: Dictators, Despots, and Tyrants*, Lanham, Maryland: Rowman and Littlefield, 2006

Li Zhisui, *The Private Life of Chairman Mao*, translated by Tai Hung-Chao, New York: Random House, 1994

Ludwig, Emil, *Three Portraits: Hitler, Mussolini, Stalin*, New York: Longmans, Green and Co., 1940

Ma'oz, Moshe, *Asad: The Sphinx of Damascus*, London: Weidenfeld and Nicolson, 1988

Machiavelli, Niccolo, *The Prince*, translated by G. Bull, London: Penguin Books, 1970

Madriaga, Isabel de, *Ivan the Terrible*, New Haven: Yale University Press, 2006

Maser, Werner, *Hitler: Legend, Myth and Reality*, translated by Peter and Betty Ross, New York: Harper and Row, 1973

Massie, Allan, *Nero's Heirs*, London: Hodder and Stoughton, 1999

Massie, Allan, *Caligula*, London: Sceptre, 2004

Massie, Robert K., *Peter the Great: His Life and World*, New York: Alfred A. Knopf, 1980

Miller, Alice, *For Your Own Good: Hidden Cruelty in Child-Rearing and the Roots of Violence*, London: Virago, 1987

Miller, Judith, and Laurie Mylroie, *Saddam Hussein and the Crisis in the Gulf*, New York: Times Books, 1990

Oppenheim, Walter, *Europe and the Enlightened Despots*, London: Hodder Arnold, 1990

Ornes, Germán E., *Trujillo: Little Caesar of the Caribbean*, New York: Thomas Nelson, 1958

Overy, Richard, *The Dictators: Hitler's Germany and Stalin's Russia*, London: Book Club Associates, 2004

Pavlov, Andrei and Maureen Perrie, *Ivan the Terrible*, London: Longman, 2003

Paykel, E.S., editor, *Handbook of Affective Disorders*, New York: Guilford Press, 1982

Payne, Stanley, *History of Fascism, 1914–1945*, London: Routledge, 1996

Platt, Richard, *Julius Caesar: Great Dictator of Rome*, London: Dorling Kindersley, 2003

Preston, Paul, *Franco: A Biography*, London: Fontana, 1995

Rauschning, Hermann, *Hitler Speaks: A Series of Political Conversations with Adolf Hitler on His Real Aims*, London: Eyre and Spottiswoode, 1940

Rengger, Johan, *The Reign of Doctor Joseph Gaspard Roderick de Francia of Paraguay*, Port Washington: Kennikat Press, 1971

Richardson, Rosamond, *Stalin's Shadow: Inside the Family of One of the World's Greatest Tyrants*, New York: St Martin's Press, 1994

Ross, Terrill, *Mao: A Biography*, New York: Harper and Row, 1980

Shirer, William, *The Rise and Fall of the Third Reich: A History of Nazi Germany*, New York: Simon and Schuster, 1962

Smith, Edward, *The Young Stalin: The Early Years of an Elusive Revolutionary*, London: Cassell, 1968

Snow, Edgar, *Red Star Over China*, London: Penguin Books, 1972

Stefoff, Rebecca, *Pol Pot*, New York: Chelsea House Publishers, 1991

Suetonius, *The Twelve Caesars*, translated by Robert Graves, London: Penguin Classics, 2003

Thomas, Hugh, *The Spanish Civil War*, London: Penguin Books, 2003

Toland, John, *Adolf Hitler, Vol I, II*, New York: Doubleday and Co., 1976

Trevor-Roper, Hugh, *The Last Days of Hitler*, London: Macmillan, 1947

Trow, M.J., *Vlad the Impaler: In Search of the Real Dracula*, Gloucestershire: History Press, 2003

Tucker, Robert C., *Political Culture and Leadership in Soviet Russia: From Lenin to Gorbachev*, New York: W.W. Norton, 1988

Tucker, Robert C., *Stalin in Power: The Revolution from Above, 1928–1941*, New York: W.W. Norton, 1992

Von Papen, Franz, *Memoirs*, translated by Brian Connell, New York: Dutton and Co., 1953

Von Ribbentrop, Joachim, *The Ribbentrop Memoirs*, translated by Oliver Watson, London: Weidenfeld and Nicolson, 1954

Waite, Robert G.L., *The Psychopathic God: Adolf Hitler*, New York: Basic Books, 1977

Wilkinson, Richard, *France and Louis XIII 1661–1715*, London: Hodder Arnold, 1993

Wilson, Dick, *The People's Emperor: A Biography of Mao Tse-Tung*, New York: Doubleday and Co., 1980

Wilson, Edward Osborne, *On Human Nature*, London: Penguin Books, 2001

INDEX OF NAMES

SOME AUTHORS WE HAVE PUBLISHED

James Agee • Bella Akhmadulina • Tariq Ali • Kenneth Allsop • Alfred Andersch
Guillaume Apollinaire • Machado de Assis • Miguel Angel Asturias • Duke of Bedford
Oliver Bernard • Thomas Blackburn • Jane Bowles • Paul Bowles • Richard Bradford
Ilse, Countess von Bredow • Lenny Bruce • Finn Carling • Blaise Cendrars • Marc Chagall
Giorgio de Chirico • Uno Chiyo • Hugo Claus • Jean Cocteau • Albert Cohen
Colette • Ithell Colquhoun • Richard Corson • Benedetto Croce • Margaret Crosland
e.e. cummings • Stig Dalager • Salvador Dalí • Osamu Dazai • Anita Desai
Charles Dickens • Bernard Diederich • Fabián Dobles • William Donaldson
Autran Dourado • Yuri Druzhnikov • Lawrence Durrell • Isabelle Eberhardt
Sergei Eisenstein • Shusaku Endo • Erté • Knut Faldbakken • Ida Fink
Wolfgang George Fischer • Nicholas Freeling • Philip Freund • Carlo Emilio Gadda
Rhea Galanaki • Salvador Garmendia • Michel Gauquelin • André Gide
Natalia Ginzburg • Jean Giono • Geoffrey Gorer • William Goyen • Julien Gracq
Sue Grafton • Robert Graves • Angela Green • Julien Green • George Grosz
Barbara Hardy • H.D. • Rayner Heppenstall • David Herbert • Gustaw Herling
Hermann Hesse • Shere Hite • Stewart Home • Abdullah Hussein • King Hussein of Jordan
Ruth Inglis • Grace Ingoldby • Yasushi Inoue • Hans Henny Jahnn • Karl Jaspers
Takeshi Kaiko • Jaan Kaplinski • Anna Kavan • Yasunuri Kawabata • Nikos Kazantzakis
Orhan Kemal • Christer Kihlman • James Kirkup • Paul Klee • James Laughlin
Patricia Laurent • Violette Leduc • Lee Seung-U • Vernon Lee • József Lengyel
Robert Liddell • Francisco García Lorca • Moura Lympany • Thomas Mann
Dacia Maraini • Marcel Marceau • André Maurois • Henri Michaux • Henry Miller
Miranda Miller • Marga Minco • Yukio Mishima • Quim Monzó • Margaret Morris
Angus Wolfe Murray • Atle Næss • Gérard de Nerval • Anaïs Nin • Yoko Ono
Uri Orlev • Wendy Owen • Arto Paasilinna • Marco Pallis • Oscar Parland
Boris Pasternak • Cesare Pavese • Milorad Pavic • Octavio Paz • Mervyn Peake
Carlos Pedretti • Dame Margery Perham • Graciliano Ramos • Jeremy Reed
Rodrigo Rey Rosa • Joseph Roth • Ken Russell • Marquis de Sade • Cora Sandel
Iván Sándor • George Santayana • May Sarton • Jean-Paul Sartre
Ferdinand de Saussure • Gerald Scarfe • Albert Schweitzer
George Bernard Shaw • Isaac Bashevis Singer • Patwant Singh • Edith Sitwell
Suzanne St Albans • Stevie Smith • C.P. Snow • Bengt Söderbergh
Vladimir Souloukhin • Natsume Soseki • Muriel Spark • Gertrude Stein • Bram Stoker
August Strindberg • Rabindranath Tagore • Tambimuttu • Elisabeth Russell Taylor
Emma Tennant • Anne Tibble • Roland Topor • Miloš Urban • Anne Valery
Peter Vansittart • José J. Veiga • Tarjei Vesaas • Noel Virtue • Max Weber
Edith Wharton • William Carlos Williams • Phyllis Willmott
G. Peter Winnington • Monique Wittig • A.B. Yehoshua • Marguerite Young
Fakhar Zaman • Alexander Zinoviev • Emile Zola

 Peter Owen Publishers, 81 Ridge Road, London N8 9NP, UK
T + 44 (0)20 8350 1775 / E info@peterowen.com
www.peterowen.com / @PeterOwenPubs
Independent publishers since 1951